ADVANCED CONVERSATION

Marion Geddes
Gill Sturtridge
Sheila Been

PHOENIX
ELT
incorporating
PRENTICE HALL MACMILLAN

Published 1995 by Phoenix ELT
Campus 400, Spring Way
Maylands Avenue, Hemel Hempstead
Hertfordshire, HP2 7EZ

A division of Prentice Hall International (UK) Ltd

First Published 1991 by Macmillan Publishers Limited

Illustrations by Helen Ganly
Produced by AMR

Printed in Malaysia

A catalogue record for this book is available from the British Library

ISBN 0-13-547366-7

7 6 5 4

1999 98 97 96

The authors and publishers would like to thank the following photographic sources:

Greg Evans Photo Library p.43; Mary Evans Picture Library p.66; Rex Features p.59; The Kobal Collection p.63.

The authors and publishers also wish to thank the following who have kindly given permission for the use of copyright material:

Collins English Dictionaries for two entries from *Collins English Dictionary, 3rd edition*, 1991 (page 34).

Cressrelles Publishing Company Ltd. for an extract from *Do You Take This Woman: And Other Disasters* by Colin Reid (page 73).

Curtis Brown Group Ltd. on behalf of Robert Morley for an abridged extract from *Robert Morley's Book of Worries*, published by Weidenfeld Publishers Ltd. (page 53).

Mary Glasgow Publications Ltd. for the article 'Balancing on the edges of Language' by David Crystal from *Practical English Teaching*, December 1986 (pages 81 & 87).

David Higham Associates Ltd. on behalf of the Estate of Dylan Thomas for an extract from *Memories of Childhood*, published by J. M. Dent & Sons Ltd. (pages 91).

The Right Hon. the Earl of Longford for his article 'The present prison system should be abolished' published in *Living*, April/May 1984 (page 59).

Octopus Children's Publishing for the poem 'Sneezles' from *Now We Are Six* by A. A. Milne, published by Methuen Children's Books (page 33).

Peters Fraser & Dunlop Ltd. on behalf of Nigel Rees for an extract from *The Joy Of Clichés*, published by Macdonald & Company (page 52).

Random Century Group for an extract from *Right Ho, Jeeves* by P. G. Wodehouse (page 50) published by Hutchinson Publishers, and for 'About Friends' from *Spitfire On The Northern Line* by Brian Jones, published by Chatto & Windus Ltd. (page 23).

Every effort has been made to trace all the copyright holders but if any have been inadvertently overlooked, the publishers will be pleased to make the necessary arrangement at the first opportunity.

CONTENTS

CONTENTS

ABOUT THIS BOOK

Aims

This book will help you to:

- practise speaking with greater grammatical accuracy;
- improve your pronunciation;
- practise speaking with confidence and fluency on a variety of topics and in a variety of situations;
- extend your linguistic repertoire;
- enrich your vocabulary;
- become more aware of language and thereby improve your communicative ability on your own.

You have reached an advanced level in your English and so you can already speak with considerable fluency and accuracy. This book gives practice therefore in additional skills:

- reading aloud effectively
- interpreting in both English and your mother tongue
- speaking in more stressful situations than you may have previously experienced, e.g. making a speech

Outline

The **Introduction : Thinking about speaking** is to help you clarify for yourself what aspects of speaking you wish to improve.

Units 1 to 6 all follow the same format.

Part 1 provides opportunities for both controlled and free practice. A variety of activities relating to the theme of the unit involve you in free conversation, discussion, giving talks and debating. You also practise language functions particularly useful in controlling conversation and discussion.

Part 2 includes exercises in pronunciation, vocabulary, reading aloud, and interpretation. The exercise types may be unfamiliar to you and so they are described in detail in **Unfamiliar exercises**, below.

Postscript gives some suggestions for ways of improving your English on your own at the end of your language course.

Unfamiliar exercises

1 Shadow reading

'Shadow reading' is reading aloud with a tape recording, following the pace, rhythm, and intonation of the recorded speaker. Shadow reading exercises help you:

- improve your pronunciation and intonation
- speak with more expression
- speak more flowingly

Shadow reading is best done in a language laboratory, where you can work on your own at your own pace and you can compare your speech with the speech on the tape.

If your school or college does not have a language laboratory or a mini-lab, then the best way to practise shadow reading is at home, with your own copy of the tape material.

Procedure

Each exercise consists of a recording and a transcript of it in the book. The procedure for each exercise is the same.

1 Skim (read quickly) through the transcript to see what it is about. Check the meaning of anything you are not sure about, by asking your teacher or by using a dictionary. Then, in pencil, mark up the transcript in any way that you think will help you read it aloud. You can mark for example:

– pauses for breathing or dramatic effect /

– longer pauses for dramatic effect //

– stressed syllables: a<u>bove</u>, discrimi<u>na</u>tion

– catenation (linking of words): this afternoon

– intonation patterns: ╲ falling; ╱ rising

– pace: 〰〰 fast; ⁓⁓ slower

On page 25 there is a text marked up in this way.

2 Listen to the recording and at the same time follow the transcript silently. This time, in ink (or another colour), mark the transcript according to how it is spoken in the recording. Compare the markings. Are there many differences? Where do most of the differences lie? For example in stress, intonation, catenation, pauses, or pace?

3 Rewind the tape to the beginning of the text. If you are working in a language laboratory, adjust your machine so that you are in 'Record'. Lower the 'master' volume slightly. Try 'shadowing' the voice on the tape by reading the transcript aloud at the same time and in the same manner as the recorded voice. Work at this, rewinding and re-recording as much as you wish.

If you are working with a tape recorder, you will not be able to record your own voice - unless of course you use a second tape recorder.

2 Word study

To do the exercises in this section, you should have available as many different kinds of dictionary as you can lay your hands on. In this way you will become familiar with a number of reference works and find out their respective weaknesses and strengths. You should also spend some time thinking about the best techniques for noting down and reviewing new words and phrases and their meanings.

You should already be familiar with at least one of these dictionaries:

Oxford Advanced Learner's Dictionary of Current English
Longman Dictionary of Contemporary English
Websters English Dictionary
Collins COBUILD English Language Dictionary
Collins English Dictionary

Dictionaries that you may be less familiar with include:

Dictionary of Link Words, Macmillan
English Prepositional Idioms, Macmillan
Dictionary of Everyday Idioms, Macmillan
A Student's Dictionary of Phrasal Verbs, Macmillan
Oxford Dictionary of Current Idiomatic English (2 volumes)
Longman Dictionary of English Idioms
Longman Lexicon of Contemporary English
The Pan Dictionary of Synonyms and Antonyms
Dictionary of Confusing Words and Meanings, Routledge and Kegan Paul
Dictionary of Contrasting Pairs, Routledge
Cassell's Modern Guide to Synonyms and Related Words
Roget's Thesaurus

3 Reading Aloud

Reading aloud to friends and family is something that is part of everyday life: items from the newspaper, extracts from letters we have received, bedtime stories and so on. Many professionals also have to read aloud as part of their work: teachers, business people, lawyers, etc. Reading aloud is therefore an appropriate skill for you to master.

When you are doing Reading Aloud exercises, remember you are reading for the benefit or entertainment of your listener. (This is where the activity of reading-round-the-class that you may have done when you first started learning English breaks down. There is no apparent audience: the task is simply to read aloud - and not to read *to someone*.)

Hints

Reading aloud is not silent reading made audible. However informal, however intimate the situation may be, it is still a theatrical activity of some sort. Here are some hints to help you.

1 Open the mouth and jaw: let the sound out.
2 Speak up sufficiently to reach your listener(s).
3 Don't be afraid to gesture when it seems natural.
4 Vary the volume, pace, pitch and tone as the sense dictates.
5 Don't be afraid to pause.
6 Hold the book up; don't read to the floor but look up at your listener(s) as much as possible and make eye-contact.
7 Hold the book in your left hand so that your right hand is free to turn the page.

When doing Shadow Reading exercises, you follow the voice on the tape, imitating pauses, pace, pronunciation, intonation etc. In Reading Aloud exercises you decide these features for yourself. Before you read, mark up the text using the notation suggested in **Shadow reading**, page 6.

4 Interpreting

Most of the exercises in this book practise *liaison interpreting* (as opposed to *consecutive* and *simultaneous interpreting*).

Liaison interpreting is what you sometimes have to do when hosting a foreign visitor. You interpret for members of your family who do not understand your visitor's language, and you interpret for your visitor when, for example, you and your family are watching a TV programme in your mother tongue, or when you take your visitor on a sightseeing tour with a guide speaking your mother tongue. You may have to do some liaison interpreting when you help tourists who are having problems making themselves understood at a hotel or in the street, or when there are people of different nationalities at a party.

Interpreting in the language classroom is obviously an artificial exercise. You have to create the 'dramatic illusion' that an interpreter is required, and it is important that this illusion is not broken by someone interrupting to correct a mistake. So how can mistakes be corrected?

The students taking part in the exercise can be responsible for some of the correction. For example, grammatical and pronunciation mistakes can be corrected on the spot by the student who is being given the interpretation, just as might happen in a real interpreting situation. When the interpreter mis-interprets what has been said, the student (who in reality has understood the message without interpretation) can refuse to understand what is being said by the interpreter.

The teacher can also help in correction. For example, the teacher (or student monitors) can keep a note of mistakes made and report them at the end of the activity. Alternatively, the teacher may be able to record (part of) the exercise and play it back later, stopping the tape to comment on mistakes.

In Units 3, 4, and 6 the Interpreting exercises are based on recorded material. These exercises are best done in the language laboratory (unless you are using video in Unit 6).

In the language laboratory, work straight through the whole exercise without stopping the tape. Rewind and listen to yourself, noticing where you could improve your interpretation. Then do the exercise again.

If there is only one tape-recorder for the whole class, the teacher will nominate individual students to interpret each section. Before moving on to the next section, the class will discuss the interpretation that has just been made and, if necessary, another student will try interpreting the same section again.

If two tape recorders are available, one can be used to record individual students' interpretations. Discussion can either take place after each section or be left till the end of the exercise.

If several tape recorders are available, make copies of the exercise and work in small groups with a tape recorder for each group.

Hints

When you are doing liaison interpreting remember:

1 You are not trying to translate phrase by phrase or sentence by sentence. Rather, your job is to ensure that the communicative intention of one speaker is fully conveyed to the other. Your interpretation will often be only about two thirds the length of the original utterance.
2 You may sometimes have to extract from a relatively rambling statement the essential gist of what has been said.
3 If you can't find the exact word or phrase to interpret something, try to find other ways to express what you want to say.

We hope that you find these and all the other exercises in this book interesting - and worthwhile. Good luck!

Marion Geddes Gill Sturtridge Sheila Been

THINKING ABOUT SPEAKING

'All life comes back to the question of our speech, the medium through which we communicate with each other; for all life comes back to the question of our relations with one another.'

Henry James

This book is for advanced students. This means that you have already achieved a considerable degree of fluency and can express yourself well and accurately in English. So what more do you want?

It is important for you to think about this question before you start working with this book. Your answers will help you appreciate the aims of the varied activities in the book, and help you think carefully about what you want to get out of them and how your teacher and your fellow-students can help you.

1 A student talks about her spoken English

To begin with you are going to hear Wanda, a student from France, talk about her English and why she wants to improve it.

Listen to her and answer these questions:

1 What aspects of her spoken English does Wanda want to improve?
2 What does she do to improve her vocabulary?
3 What is her overall aim in trying to improve her spoken English?

Do you share any of Wanda's feelings about speaking English?

2 Your attitudes to speaking English

Discuss these statements in groups for about five minutes. Share with the rest of the class the most interesting or controversial point(s) that have come out of your discussion.

1 I want to speak English with a perfect native-speaker accent.
2 I want to speak English without a single grammatical mistake.
3 I must enlarge my vocabulary in order to improve my spoken English.
4 I feel as though I am a different person when I speak English.
5 If I read English, my spoken English will benefit as well.
6 The best way to improve my spoken English is quite simply to speak, as often as possible, to as many different people as possible.
7 I don't speak as much as I would like to because I'm afraid of making mistakes.
8 I don't like working in groups because I may learn incorrect English from my classmates.

3 *Working with this book*

Read **About this book - Aims** on page 5. What are the aims of this book? Which ones will be most useful to you? Why?

4 *Working on your own*

As you have seen, one of the aims of this book is to extend your linguistic repertoire. This is something you should also be doing on your own.

1 Find new ways of saying things.

You may have 'favoured phrases' - vocabulary and grammatical structures which you feel confident with and use in preference to alternatives which have the same meaning. For example:

a These three sentences have the same meaning.

1 *If the chairman resigned, I would too.*
2 *Suppose the chairman were to resign, I would too.*
3 *Were the chairman to resign, I would too.*

However, many learners favour the structure '*If* + past tense' and never use the structures in 2 and 3.

b Similarly, all these phrases can be used to compliment someone.

What a lovely dress!
I like your dress!
That dress looks very nice on you!
You look lovely in that dress!
That dress really suits you!

Many learners use only one or two of them.

Are you aware of any 'favoured phrases' that you have or phrases and structures that you try to avoid using?

2 Carry a notebook around with you to note any interesting language you come across.

You can use your notebook in two ways. Sometimes focus on particular language, for example the language used in greetings or to close a conversation, or to make a request. At other times, simply note down anything you come across that interests you.

Bring your discoveries to class and share them with other students.

At the end of this book, in **Postscript** (page 76 - 79), you will find further suggestions for ways of improving your English on your own.

unit 1

USING LANGUAGE TO BE SOCIABLE

PART ONE

'The ability to chat, to exchange amicable conversational turns with another speaker, forms the basis of our social life.'

G Brown et al. Teaching Talk

1.1 Encouraging conversation

1.1 Task 1

To encourage conversation, it is important to be a good *listener* as well as a good speaker. When we are listening, we can show our interest *non-verbally*, by nodding our heads, raising our eyebrows, laughing and so on. We can also show our interest *verbally*.

Listen to this conversation and notice how the woman verbally encourages the man to keep talking.

	Man	D'you know, today is the tenth anniversary of my arrival in Britain.
Makes a comment	**Woman**	Really!
	Man	Yes, I was brought up in the Soviet Union. I lived there for the first twenty years of my life.
Makes a comment	**Woman**	How interesting!
	Man	I was born in Siberia.
Asks a short question	**Woman**	Were you?
	Man	Yes, my parents went to live there in 1958 and stayed for about eight years. What I remember best are the winters. Terribly cold - the temperature goes down to minus fifty degrees.
Repeats a key word/phrase	**Woman**	Minus fifty!
	Man	It can be pretty awful.
Rephrases a key word/phrase	**Woman**	Horrible.
	Man	And I remember snow storms that went on for days on end. And the winter itself is very long.
Asks for more information	**Woman**	How long?
	Man	Oh, about five or six months. But you know, I think winter is my favourite season of the year.

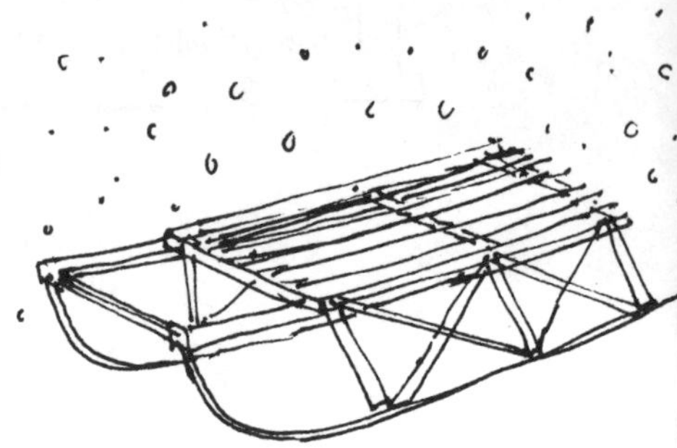

Asks for more information	**Woman**	What makes you say that?
	Man	Well, we used to go tobogganing for example.
Asks for an explanation	**Woman**	What's that?
	Man	Sledging.
Asks for an explanation	**Woman**	Sorry, I don't know that word.
	Man	Oh, sorry. I'll draw you a picture. Look, this is a sledge.
Makes a comment	**Woman**	Oh, of course. Yes, sledging's great fun.

Now play the part of the woman. You will hear the conversation again on the cassette, but this time the woman's voice is missing. You can speak when the tape is silent. Try to do this with your book closed.

1.1 Task 2

In the next conversation, a man is telling a friend about his work as a tourist guide, taking people round Windsor Castle.

Listen once without looking at the transcript. As you listen

1 notice how the woman continually encourages the man to keep talking.

2 write down three things that tourists told or asked the man.

Rewind the tape and listen again. This time complete the transcript.

Man Do you know I used to work as a tourist guide?

Woman Yes I remember that.

Man Yes that's right, it was about two years ago, um I did it for about a year -

Woman That's right.

Man - and I finished two years ago. One of the things I had to do was take people around Windsor Castle, which is, you know, the Queen's weekend residence outside London.

Woman Yes, ...

Man And I used to have to take people round it, show them the sights (**Woman** Uhum.) and er explain it to them as much as I possibly could. But some of the strangest things used to happen, especially with American tourists.

Woman ....

Man Occasionally, as you can imagine, it was it was -

Woman Weird questions.

Man - strange, the questions you used to get. Once I had a professor, and I didn't know he was a professor, and I was telling them about the date of something or other -

Woman Right.

Man - and er he said 'No, you've got that wrong'.

Woman Oh no.

Man I think it was, it was awful, it was really embarrassing.

Woman ....

Man Oh he was right -

Woman Gosh.

Man - he was right because I, I guessed, I'd forgotten I'm ashamed to say and I was stupid enough to think 'Oh well, they probably won't know, I'll just tell them anyway. And he said 'No, you've got that wrong. Queen Elizabeth was born in 1536.'

Woman ....!

Man It was, it really was. I had to er speak very fast to cover up for it.

Woman I can imagine.

Man But other times you get the very very stupidest comments, I mean really, really embarrassing sometimes (**Woman** *laughs*) or, or um funny, you have to keep a straight face.

Woman ....?

Man Well once I was telling them something, we were on the terrace outside the castle looking out over the Thames Valley -

Woman Oh, how ....!

Man Oh it is, it's a wonderful view. Have you seen it?

Woman Yes I have, it's ....

Man And we were looking out over there and an aeroplane came over because Heathrow, as you probably know, is is only about five miles away -

Woman Yes, that's right.

Man - um, and the aeroplanes are landing every two minutes (**Woman** Uhum.) or something like that. And this aeroplane came over making a terrible noise and I had to stop speaking. And when the sound of the aeroplane had died away one of the tourists said to me, she said 'Why did the Queen build her castle so close to the airport?'

Woman (*laughs*) Oh no! I mean ....to that sort of comment?

Man I don't know. I just, I just had to try and not laugh and keep a straight face, it was very difficult.

Woman Oh no!

Man And er sometimes I had to explain to them about what was inside in the State Apartments.

Woman Oh, they're ....! I-

Man They are, they're lovely, aren't they.

Woman .... , yes.

Man With all the tapestries and paintings -

Woman And jewels as well.

Man - and furniture. The jewels are lovely as well, although there's more at the Tower of London than -

Woman Yes of course.

Man - than, than at Windsor. But I would have to explain to them, and then they'd get everything mixed up.

Woman I can imagine.

Man So they'd think that the portrait of Queen Elizabeth was Queen Mary and, and they'd think that this room was that room and er, I'd have, I'd have to do more explaining when they got out. Another time when they came out it was pouring with rain -

Woman .... !

Man Yes, as usual, you know, and er somebody came up to me and said 'Why have you made it rain?'

Woman ....

Man I know, it's incredible isn't it. And I said 'There's many things I can do but that I can't do.'

Woman Stopping it rain is not one of them.

Man No. That's right. You can't have a private telephone line to God.

Woman .... , though.

Man Yes. Yes. Very enjoyable. You're always on the move, always in different places, going round beautiful historic places.

Woman And meeting er interesting people.

Man Yes.

1.1 Task 3

Work in twos.

A tells **B** about something, e.g. a wonderful childhood memory, your country (e.g. interesting customs, geography, politics), how and where you have learned English, an interesting/frightening experience, what you did last night, what you are planning to do tomorrow, a book you are reading, etc. Talk for about one minute.

B is a good listener and encourages **A** by using some of the devices listed in Task 1. Use as many as you can.

Take it in turns to be **A** and **B**.

1.2 Redirecting the conversation

1.2 Task 1

To redirect a conversation, you can often pick up a word or phrase that has just been used and say:

Talking of ....
Speaking ....
Talking of X makes me think of ....
That reminds me. That reminds me of ....
Incidentally ....

For example:

A I went with Rachel to that new Indian **restaurant** on Sunday. It was her birthday.

B (*encouraging*) Really? (*redirecting*) **That reminds me**, did you know that a very good Sri Lankan **restaurant** has just opened in my neighbourhood?

or: **Incidentally**, I've just come back from Scotland. You can find Chinese **restaurants** all over the place there.

or: **Talking of eating**, did you know that people in Papua New Guinea eat ants? I was reading about it last night.

A (*encouraging*) How interesting.

Notice that sometimes you may change the form of the word, e.g. restaurant - restaurants, or use an associated word, e.g. restaurant - eating

Work in pairs. **A** starts each time by using these sentences:

1 Yesterday I spent practically the whole evening watching **a cricket match** on television. I didn't get much work done.

2 I spent all Wednesday afternoon going to one **shop** after another, but finally I found a present for my mother.

3 My nephew is very **musical**. He already plays the piano and now he's learning the guitar.

4 Red's my **favourite** colour. That's why I bought roses. They're lovely, aren't they?

5 My cousin was feeling a bit **lonely** last Sunday, so we went out to the cinema together. We saw a terrific film. You must see it.

1.2 Task 2

Work in groups of three or four. **A** starts a conversation by making a statement. **B** redirects the conversation by picking up a word or phrase that **A** has just used. **C** redirects the conversation again by picking up something **B** has said, and so on. Try to keep going for two or three minutes.

1.2 Task 3

In groups of three or four, have a ten minute conversation about one of the questions below. Remember to encourage each other to talk. Don't be afraid to redirect the conversation by using some of the phrases in Task 1.

The purpose of this task is to make sure that:

1 everyone in the group is drawn into the conversation,

2 everyone listens to whoever is talking,
3 no-one dominates the conversation,
4 the conversation flows easily from one associated idea to another.

Questions

a) Does television discourage or encourage conversation in the home?
b) What are the 'blood pressure' subjects in your home?
c) Do you enjoy an evening on your own at home?
d) Which household tasks do you enjoy doing? Which do you dislike?
e) If you were suddenly given a gift of £5000, what would you do with it?

1.3 It's not what you say, but how you say it

1.3 Task 1

On the cassette you can hear a conversation between a husband and his wife. The husband does most of the talking. The wife only says 'Yes, dear' - four times. As you listen, draw a line through her words to illustrate the intonation pattern and the pitch range she uses each time she speaks. For example:

Yes, dear. (falling intonation with a small pitch range)

Yes, dear. (rising intonation with a wide pitch range)

1. Yes, dear. 2. Yes, dear. 3. Yes, dear. 4. Yes, dear.

Think about pace. In which 'yes, dear' is the pace quickest? And in which is it slowest?

Rewind the cassette and listen again. This time pause after each 'Yes, dear' and guess what the wife is really 'saying'.

1.3 Task 2

Look at the transcript. In pairs, read the conversation aloud, paying particular attention to intonation, tone of voice and pace. The parts in parenthesis ( ) are to help you decide how the lines should be spoken. Do not read them aloud.

Husband Mary dear. (*I expect my wife to look after me a bit better than this.*)

Wife Yes, dear. (*I'm a good, hard-working wife.*)

Husband Is my green tie in the wardrobe? (*I know it isn't, but I'll give her a chance to explain why it isn't there.*)

Wife Yes, dear. (*I don't understand. Why doesn't he look for it himself?*)

Husband Well, I can't find it there, and this is the third time running my tie isn't where it should be. (*I don't enjoy having to tell you, but I have no choice.*)

Wife Yes, dear. (*Here we go again.*)

Husband Come here and find it for me. I simply can't go on hunting for it any longer. (*What are wives for, if not to look after their husbands?*)

Wife Yes, dear. (*Why didn't you ask me in the first place - a little more politely - instead of going through all this rigmarole?*)

1.3 Task 3

Work in pairs. Write another conversation like the one in Task 2, where the second person repeats the same phrase. The conversation could be between a teacher and a student, a boss and his/her secretary, a shop manager and assistant, or a clerk and an office boy.

Exchange your written conversations with another pair and practise reading the new one aloud. Ask the other pair for help if you have any problems with intonation or tone of voice.

1.4 Thinking about error correction

In the activities you have been doing in this unit, you probably made some mistakes - in grammar, pronunciation and vocabulary. Perhaps, also, you were able to communicate what you wanted, but you were aware that it could have been done in a better way.

What happened to these mistakes or inadequacies?

– Were most of them corrected? Did you want them to be corrected?

– Who corrected them? Yourself? A fellow-student? Your teacher?

Here is a list of techniques teachers may use to correct their students' mistakes. Did your teacher use any of these? Or any other techniques?

Rate each technique on a scale 1 to 5, where 1 is a technique you like very much and 5 is a technique you do not like at all. Explain why you chose each rating.

1 Your teacher indicated that a mistake had been made but didn't correct it. This was done either non-verbally (e.g. by frowning) or verbally (e.g. 'What was that?', 'Sorry, what did you say?')

2 Your teacher drew attention to the mistake by repeating the mistake with a questioning intonation (e.g. 'He *say*?')

3 Your teacher gave the correct version immediately after you had made the mistake

4 Your teacher wrote a list of (some of) the mistakes made by various members of the class and then went through them at the end of the activity.

5 Your teacher wrote down students' individual mistakes on small cards and silently handed them to the student concerned during the activity. At the end of the activity the teacher went through the mistakes with the students.

6 Your speech was recorded and analysed later for mistakes.

7 Your mistakes were ignored.

Should it always be the teacher who corrects, or is it useful to have students as 'correction monitors' sometimes, e.g. during a discussion?

Is it useful to have 'accuracy periods' (say, ten minutes) when mistakes will be carefully monitored?

Is it useful sometimes to focus only on certain types of mistake, e.g. articles or tenses?

PART TWO

2.1 Shadow reading: awkward encounters

2.1 Task 1

In this section you are going to do some 'shadow reading'. Read the section in **About this book - Shadow reading**, page 6, which explains how shadow reading can help you and what you should do.

2.1 Task 2

As you have just read, one of the purposes of shadow reading is to improve your pronunciation. Many of the pronunciation problems you may have are probably typical of speakers of your mother tongue. For example, Japanese speakers find it difficult to distinguish between 'r' and 'l' because neither of these sounds exist in their language.

Make a list of some of the pronunciation problems typical of speakers of your language. Compare your list with other students in the class.

2.1 Task 3

Shadow read these texts.

1 Conversing with Queen Victoria

Queen Victoria reigned for more than sixty years from 1837 to 1901. This text describes the scene after a formal dinner at the palace where the Queen is socializing with her dinner guests.

When the company was reassembled in the drawing-room the etiquette was stiff. For a few minutes the Queen spoke in turn to each of her guests; and during these short uneasy colloquies the aridity of royalty was apt to become painfully evident. One night Mr Greville, the Clerk of the Privy Council, was present; his turn soon came; the middle-aged hard-faced viveur was addressed by his young hostess.

'Have you been riding today, Mr Greville?' asked the Queen.

'No, Madam, I have not,' replied Mr Greville.

'It was a fine day,' continued the Queen.

'Yes, Madam, a very fine day,' said Mr Greville.

'It was rather cold, though,' said the Queen.

'It was rather cold, Madam,' said Mr Greville.

'Your sister, Lady Francis Egerton, rides, I think, doesn't she?' said the Queen.

'She does ride sometimes, Madam,' said Mr Greville.

There was a pause, after which Mr Greville ventured to take the lead, though he did not venture to change the subject.

'Has your Majesty been riding today?' asked Mr Greville.

'Oh yes, a very long ride,' answered the Queen with animation.

'Has your Majesty got a nice horse?' said Mr Greville.

'Oh a very nice horse,' said the Queen.

It was over. Her Majesty gave a smile and an inclination of the head, Mr Greville a profound bow, and the next conversation began with the next gentleman.

2 About Friends

The good thing about friends
is not having to finish sentences.
I sat a whole summer afternoon with my friend once
on a river bank, basking heels on the baked mud
and watching the small chunks slide into the water
and listening to them - plop plop plop.
He said 'I like the twigs when they...you know...
like that'. I said 'There's that branch...'
We both said 'Mmmm'. The river flowed and flowed
and there were lots of butterflies, that afternoon.

I first thought there was a sad thing about friends
when we met twenty years later.
We both talked hundreds of sentences,
taking care to finish all we said,
and explain it all very carefully,
as if we'd been discovered in places
we should not be, and were somehow ashamed.

I understood then what the river meant by flowing.

2.1 Task 4

Look again at the exchanges between Queen Victoria and Mr Greville. Why does the conversation not develop beyond a series of simple questions and answers? What could either the Queen or Mr Greville have done to make it develop? (Think about intonation as well as verbal ways of encouraging conversation.)

2.1 Task 5

Work in pairs. Describe to each other a friend with whom you don't have to 'finish sentences'.

2.2 Word study : differences and similarities

Read **About this book - Word study**, page 7.

Work in pairs. Discuss what the differences and/or similarities in meaning are between:

a) stiff/formal
b) inclination/nod
c) profound/deep
d) basking/sun-bathing
e) slide/glide
f) plop/splash
g) ashamed/embarrassed

You will find it helpful to think of:

– contexts in which the words can/can't be used
– other words with which they can/don't collocate

2.3 Reading aloud : news snippets

2.3 Task 1

Read the section in **About this book - Reading aloud**, page 8.

2.3 Task 2

You are going to read aloud this news item. To make it easier to read, it has been reprinted below to show:

/ breathing places, where you can pause to take a breath

‿ catenation, where the end of one word glides into the next one

— stressed syllables in multi-syllable words which some students might not be sure about.

> **Tears save buffalo**
>
> HONGKONG - Workers at a Hongkong abattoir refused to slaughter a good-natured water buffalo, forcing its owner to sell the animal to a Buddhist monastery, newspapers reported yesterday. The buffalo, imported from China, knelt down on its front legs and shed tears, refusing to be dragged into the slaughterhouse. The 540kg. animal stood up only after butchers promised that it would not be killed, the reports added.

Listen to the news item being read aloud on the cassette. Then practise reading it aloud yourself.

Tears save buffalo

Workers at a Hongkong abattoir/ refused to slaughter a good-natured water buffalo,/ forcing its owner to sell the animal to a Buddhist monastery,/newspapers reported yesterday./The buffalo, imported from China,/knelt down on its front legs/and shed tears, refusing to be dragged into the slaughterhouse./The 540 (five hundred and forty) kilo animal stood up only after butchers promised that it would not be killed,/the report added.

2.3 Task 3

Work in pairs. **A** will read the newspaper items on page 80. **B** will read the newspaper items on page 86.

First, skim read your news items silently. Choose two or three items that you find interesting/amusing etc. Prepare to read them aloud by marking breathing pauses, important stressed syllables, and catenation. Think also about pace, intonation, and pronunciation.

When you have finished, catch your partner's attention and read the headline of one of the items aloud. Your partner will make an encouraging comment to show interest in hearing the whole item. Read the item to your partner.

For example:

A (catching **B**'s attention)
Listen to this, B.
What do you think of this?
Hey, have you read this?

11 YEAR OLD
AVIATOR FLIES
ACROSS THE ATLANTIC

B (encouraging **A** to read the whole item)
An eleven year old! That's a bit young, isn't it?
or *Oh, yes I heard about that on the radio. What does the paper say?*

2.3 Task 4

Decide which is the most interesting/unusual/funniest item that has been read aloud. If necessary, ask your partner to remind you of an item by reading it to you again. Compare your choice with other students.

2.3 Task 5

Look for interesting items in an English language newspaper. Bring it to class and read the items aloud to the rest of the class.

2.4 Interpreting : conversations with a visitor from abroad

2.4 Task 1

Interpreting is often associated with formal situations such as conferences and lectures. Can you think of informal situations in which people are called upon to interpret? Have you ever had to act as an interpreter, either from English into your mother tongue or vice-versa?

Read the section in **About this book - Interpreting**, (page 8).

2.4 Task 2

Have you ever been in this situation? How did it feel?

A has a foreign friend **B**, who is on a visit. Their common language is English.

C is also a friend of **A**. Their common language is their mother tongue.

C doesn't speak English so, when **A**, **B** and **C** are together, **A** has to act as interpreter.

Work in threes and act out the situation. Have a conversation with **A** as the interpreter for **B** and **C**. Talk about anything you like, for example:

A and **C** tell **B** something about their country (geography, tourist sights, customs, daily life etc.).

A and **C** make suggestions and plans for places **B** could visit.

B tells **A** and **C** about his/her country.

B asks **A** and **C** questions about their country.

A, **B** and **C** together discuss a general question such as one of those listed in Part 1.2, Task 3.

unit 2

ENJOYING LANGUAGE

PART ONE

The choice of funny or silly words, grammatical patterns, pronunciations, and tones of voice is a normal part of informal conversation. In one study of an evening's conversation, the participants 'tampered with' several linguistic features, for humorous effect : one person talked of climbing 'an Ande'; another coined a false gender, saying 'a customs officer-ess'; and a third speaker, talking about football, adopted a mock-American accent, commenting 'We wuz robbed.'

David Crystal, The Cambridge Encyclopedia of Language

1.1 Balancing on the edges of language

1.1 Task 1

In pairs, make a list of what you think are the signs of true fluency in a foreign language.

Compare your list with other students.

Do you agree with David Crystal, who writes:

> *What's the mark of true fluency in a foreign language? Speaking fast, without pauses? A wide vocabulary? Controlling complex grammatical constructions? All very important, of course - but for me, the ultimate test is whether users dare to tamper with the rules of the language, to treat it as the tool it is, to make it genuinely their own.*

1.1 Task 2

When you are discussing something you have read, you may want to refer to what the writer said. Use these phrases:

According to | *this* / *him/her* | .....

It | *says* / *makes out* | *here that ....*

What it says here is that ....

As I understand it, ...

Half the class will read part **A** of David Crystal's article *Balancing on the Edges of Language,* page 81. The rest of the class will read part **B,** page 87.

Discuss what you are reading with one or two other students who are reading the same part of the article as you.

Prepare to tell someone else what you have read about. For example, you may wish to make a few headings; think about how to explain something in simple spoken language etc.

1.1 Task 3

Find someone who has read the other half of the article. In pairs:

- tell each other what you read about.
- does anything your partner read help you to understand what you read?
- does a 'breaking of rules' similar to what David Crystal describes also happen in your mother tongue?

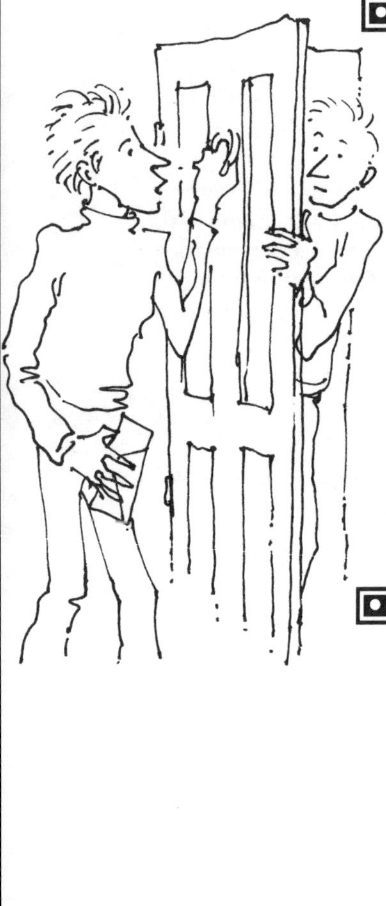

1.1 Task 4

Work in pairs. You are going to take it in turns to tell some 'Knock-Knock' jokes to each other, similar to the one David Crystal gives at the end of his article *Balancing on the Edges of Language* (Text B). You can hear it on the cassette.

A Knock knock.
B Who's there?
A Ken.
B Ken who?
A Ken't tell you.

One of you is the Comic, who starts the joke and gives the punch-line.
The other is the Feed, who encourages the Comic to give the punch-line.

A's jokes are on page 82. **B**'s jokes are on page 89.

1.1 Task 5

On the cassette you can hear this 'I don't know' joke. Listen to it and then read it aloud in pairs. Notice particularly the intonation pattern of **B**'s 'Feed' question.

A Who drives all his customers away?
B I don't know. Who *does* drive all his customers away?
A A taxi-driver.

Work in pairs. You are going to take it in turns to read some 'I don't know' jokes aloud to each other. Pay particular attention to the intonation of the 'Feed' question.

A's jokes are on page 83. **B**'s jokes are on page 90.

1.1 Task 6

These words or names all exist in English (though you may not find them all in a dictionary). Can you explain what they mean? Are any of them used in your language?

marathon *computerspeak* *user-friendly*
coffee-matic *Watergate* *racist* *Scentsational*
teleshopping *techno-phobe*

As far as we know, these words do not yet exist. What might they mean? Think of a context in which they might be used.

lecturathon *policemanspeak* *student-friendly*
ticket-a-matic *Westminstergate* *languagist* *Sightsational*
tele-exam *techno-trumpet*

1.2 Idioms

Native speakers can get their knickers in a twist when it comes to remembering idioms correctly.

Work in groups of three or four. Look at the list of statements. All of them were made on TV and radio by well-known presenters, politicians, popstars, etc. In each case one or two idioms have got confused.

What do you think the speakers were trying to say? What idiom(s) have they got confused?

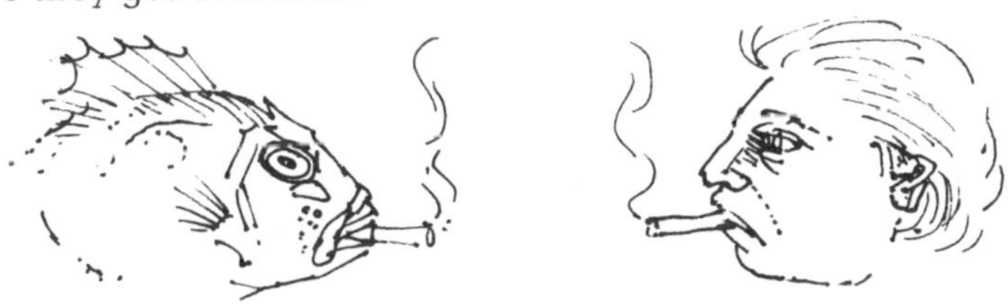

1 The pendulum has gone full circle.
2 He smokes like a fish.
3 That politician should put her voice where her mouth is.
4 Managing the Beatles was another bow to Brian Epstein's string.
5 I'm absolutely thrilled and over the world about it.
6 It was a good cricket tour to break my teeth in.

Each of you choose one of the idioms you have been discussing. (It doesn't matter if some of you choose the same idiom.) Think of a sentence in which it can be used. Then sit for a minute or two with your eyes closed trying to visualise the idiom. If you feel happy to share your image with the others in the group, describe it to them.

1.3 *A game : Call my Bluff*

1.3 Task 1

Divide into groups of three or four. Each group will be given four or five words.

Look at your words. For each word, prepare a correct definition and an example of how the word is used in a sentence. If it is used in slang or colloquially, remember to include this in your definition. (You will need to use a good English-English dictionary.) Then prepare two false, but plausible, definitions with example sentences.

1.3 Task 2

Each group tells the rest of the class which word they are going to define and then gives the three definitions and example sentences for that word. The other groups vote on which definition is the correct one. Every group that is correct gains one point.

1.4 *Expressing yourself without words*

1.4 Task 1

On the cassette you can hear two people acting out a scene. Instead of using words, they are using consecutive numbers, from 1 to 100.

First read these four scenarios. Then listen to the cassette and decide which scenario the actors are using.

Scenario 1: **A** is at home, expecting a visit from **B**. There is a knock at the dooor. It is **B**. **A** invites **B** in. Their conversation starts warmly, but moves to quarrelling or anger. Before the end of the scene (before they reach 100) they make it up and the scene finishes with their reconciliation.

Scenario 2: **A** is at home. There is an unexpected knock at the door. **A** is surprised to see **B**. Reluctantly **A** lets **B** in. Their conversation starts rather coldly but slowly becomes more friendly. By the end of the scene they are both talking animatedly and excitedly to each other.

Scenario 3: **A** is at home. **B** walks in uninvited. **A** is irritated by this and, although **B** tries to reason with **A**, **A** becomes angry. However gradually **A** calms down and by the end of the scene **A** accepts or understands **B**'s reasoning.

Scenario 4: **A** is in his/her shop. **B**, a customer, walks in. **B** complains to **A** politely. **A** refuses to accept **B**'s complaint and their conversation develops into an argument. Eventually **A** gives in to **B** and accepts **B**'s grounds for complaint. **B** politely takes leave of **A**.

1.4 Task 2

Work in pairs.

Choose one of the four scenarios and act it out in front of the class without telling the class which scenario you are using. When you have finished, the class will describe the situation they think they have witnessed and tell you which scenario they think you were using.

PART TWO

2.1 Shadow reading : poets and words

The two poems which follow both include words which the poets have invented. As you read them, enjoy the way the poets play with the sounds of English.

1 Jabberwocky

This famous poem is by Lewis Carroll, author of *Alice in Wonderland*. Some of the invented words were created by putting two words together. For example 'slithy' (line 1) means 'lithe and slimy'; 'mimsy' (line 3) means 'flimsy and miserable'. Some of the other words are names of animals which existed only in Carroll's imagination. For example a 'tove' (line 1) is a cross between a lizard, a badger and a corkscrew.

'Twas brillig and the slithy toves
Did gyre and gimble in the wabe;
All mimsy were the borogroves,
And the mome raths outgrabe.

'Beware the Jabberwock, my son!
The jaws that bite, the claws that catch!
Beware the Jubjub bird, and shun
The frumious Bandersnatch!'

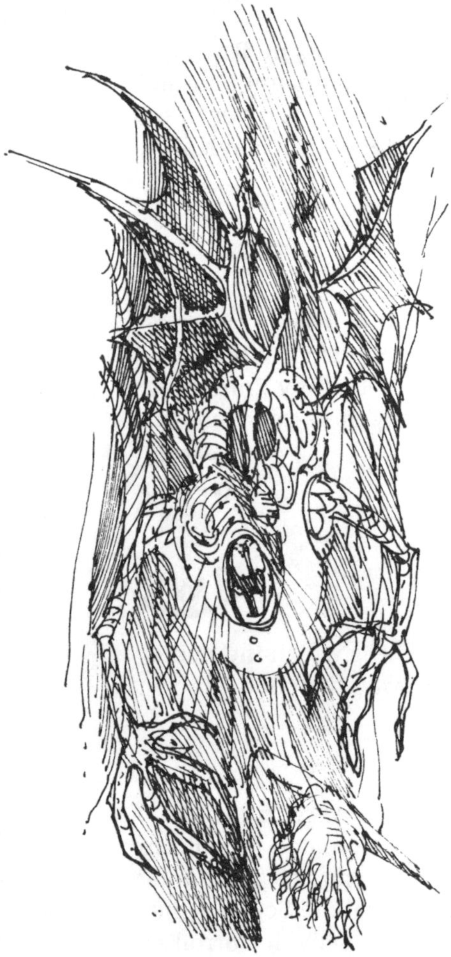

He took his vorpal sword in hand;
  Long time the manxome foe he sought -
So rested he by the Tumtum tree,
  And stood awhile in thought.

And as in uffish thought he stood,
  The Jabberwock with eyes of flame,
Came whiffling through the tulgey wood,
  And burbled as it came.

One, two! one, two! And through and through
  The vorpal blade went snicker-snack!
He left it dead, and with its head
  He went galumphing back.

'And hast thou slain the Jabberwock!
  Come to my arms, my beamish boy!
O frabjous day! Calloo! Callay!'
  He chortled in his joy.

'Twas brillig, and the slithy toves
  Did gyre and gimble in the wabe;
All mimsy were the borogroves,
  And the mome raths outgrabe.

2 Sneezles

The poem opposite is taken from a classic of children's literature: A A Milne's *Now we are six.*

Christopher Robin
Had wheezles
And sneezles.
They bundled him
Into
His bed.
They gave him what goes
With a cold in the nose,
And some more for a cold
In the head.
They wondered
If wheezles
Would turn
Into mumps;
They examined his chest
For a rash
And the rest
Of his body for swellings and lumps.
They sent for some doctors
In sneezles
And wheezles
To tell them what ought
To be done.
All sorts and conditions
Of famous physicians
Came hurrying round
At a run.
They all made a note
Of the state of his throat,
They asked if he suffered from thirst;
They asked if the sneezles
Came after the wheezles,
Or if the first sneezle
Came first.
They said 'If you teazle
A sneezle
Or wheezle,
A measle
May easily grow.
But humour or pleazle
The wheezle
Or sneezle,
The measle
Will certainly go.'
They expounded the reazles
For sneezles
And wheezles,
The manner of measles
When new.
They said 'If he freezles
In draughts and in breezles,
Then PHTHEEZLES
May even ensue.'

Christopher Robin
Got up in the morning,
The sneezles had vanished away.
And the look in his eye
Seemed to say to the sky,
'Now, how to amuse them today?'

2.2 *Word study : coined words*

2.2 Task 1

galumphing and *chortled* (verses 5 and 6 in *Jabberwocky*) have become part of the English language and are defined in dictionaries, e.g.

galumph vb. (intr.) Informal. to leap or move about clumsily or joyfully. [C19 (coined by Lewis Carroll); probably a blend of GALLOP + TRIUMPH]

chortle vb. 1. (intr.) to chuckle gleefully. n.2. a gleeful chuckle. [C19; coined (1871) by Lewis Carroll in *Through the Looking Glass*; probably a blend of CHUCKLE + SNORT]

(*Collins English Dictionary*, 1991)

Work in pairs. Discuss the similarities and differences in meaning in the words in these semantic sets:

1

move

galumph gambol hop skip leap jump

2

laugh

chortle chuckle giggle snigger titter

2.2 Task 2

Underline all the coined words in *Jabberwocky*. Although they are invented, they all sound English. Why?

Which words do you particularly like? Why? What meaning is suggested to you by these words?

Underline all the invented words in *Sneezles*. Do they remind you of real English words?

2.3 *Reading aloud : more jokes!*

Work in pairs. Practise reading aloud these jokes. Help each other decide where breathing places are and discuss intonation, catenation, stress and pronunciation.

1 A man asked his boss for a rise in salary. The boss said, 'What do you mean? Give you a rise? You don't work here at all. Listen: there are 365 days in the year - 366 this year, because it's a Leap Year. The working day is 8 hours - that's one third of a day, so over the year that's 122 days. The office is shut on Sundays so that's 52 off, making 70 days. Then you have two weeks' holiday - take off 14 days which leaves 56. There are four Bank Holidays which leaves 52. Then the office is closed on Saturdays, isn't it? Well, there are 52 Saturdays in the year - so you don't do anything here at all. Yet you're asking me for a rise!'

2 A fishmonger was painting FRESH FISH SOLD HERE TODAY above his shop when a passer-by said to him, 'You don't want to put TODAY, do you? I mean, you won't be selling it yesterday or tomorrow, will you?'

'No, I suppose not,' said the fishmonger.

'And then you don't want HERE either - you're not selling it anywhere else, are you?'

'No, that's quite right,' agreed the fishmonger.

'And then why put SOLD?' continued the helpful man. 'You're not going to give it away, are you?'

'Of course I'm not,' said the fishmonger.

'And then why say FRESH - after all you wouldn't sell it if it weren't fresh, would you?'

'I certainly wouldn't,' said the fishmonger. 'I must thank you for saving me so much trouble.'

'Just one final thing,' said the man. 'You don't need FISH either - I could smell it two streets away.'

2.4 Interpreting : helping a tourist in trouble

Work in threes.

You are going to act out a number of situations. Take it in turns to be **A**, **B** or **C**.

A is a tourist who speaks English, but not the local language.

B only speaks the local language.

C speaks English and the local language.

1 In a food shop. **B**, the shopkeeper, calls back **A**, who is just about to leave the shop with two bars of chocolate and a can of Coca-Cola. **B** is sure **A** has paid for the chocolate but not the Coca-Cola. **A** doesn't understand what the problem is. Fortunately **C**, another customer, comes to the rescue as an interpreter.

2 In a souvenir shop. **A** can't think what to buy for friends and family back home. **B**, the shopkeeper, is ready to make some suggestions but needs the help of **C**, another customer, as interpreter.

3 In a restaurant. **A** has ordered what he/she thought was a vegetarian dish, but it seems to have bits of meat in it - and it doesn't even taste nice. **B**, the waiter, doesn't understand what the problem is. **C**, sitting at the next table, comes to the rescue.

4 In a hotel. **A** is very upset. There are cockroaches in the bedroom, the shower doesn't work properly, the room overlooks a noisy street ... **B**, the hotel receptionist, understands that **A** wants to move to a different room but doesn't understand why. **C**, a visitor in the same hotel, tries to help.

unit 3

STORY TELLING

PART ONE

As you go along you must visualise the scene, the characters, their speech, their movements. See it all happening as a coloured film in your mind. Then describe it for the audience.

C N MacKay, Speak for Yourself

1.1 Telling anecdotes

1.1 Task 1

An anecdote is a true story about something that happened to ourselves or someone we know or have been told about. People often tell anecdotes, probably because they want or need to share an event that intrigued, amused, enraged or embarrassed them. In the telling, they relive the event.

On the cassette you will hear a woman telling an anecdote.

As you listen to her, notice

1 the 'lead in': how does she inform her listener that she is about to tell an anecdote?

2 the preamble/background to the story: what information is needed to set the scene?

3 how she reports conversation: does she use direct or indirect speech?

1.1 Task 2

Here is an outline of the anecdote you have just heard.

> Browsing in a bookshop one day, a novelist noticed a woman buying a copy of his most recent book, together with an edition of Shakespeare's collected plays. As the customer approached the cash desk, the novelist stopped her and asked her if she would like him to autograph his book. The woman asked him: 'Which one?'

Work in pairs. You are going to tell anecdotes to each other, using outlines like the one you have just read. If you wish, you can pretend that the anecdote is about someone you know. Add any details you wish.

A's outlines are on page 83.
B's outlines are on page 90.

Think carefully about how you are going to tell your anecdotes:

- Try to visualise the setting and the event.
- Think of a suitable lead-in.
- Organise your preamble efficiently so that it is not too long.
- Think about how you can create mood or atmosphere to match the type of anecdote you are telling.
- Use direct speech and create character and interest through the way you use your voice.
- Plan how you are going to give the punch-line.

When you are telling your anecdote, your listeners can give you feedback using the list of hints above.

If you can think of any other anecdotes, tell them to the whole class.

1.2 Interrupting

1.2 Task 1

Listen to these phrases on the cassette.

Which ones end with a fall-rise intonation pattern?
Which ones end with a fall pattern?

Interrupting politely	*Can* *May*	*I just ask*	*a question?* *something?*
Returning to the topic	*Sorry* *Excuse me*	*(for interrupting), but ...*	

Anyway ....
In any case ....
As I was saying ....
To get back to what I was saying ....
Where was I?

Now listen and repeat the phrases.

1.2 Task 2

Play this game in groups of three or four.

A starts to tell the others about something. It can be an invented story, or something he or she did recently, or a description of the journey to school/work etc. Any of the others can interrupt to ask for more information about something. Try to interrupt as often as possible and in a variety of ways. For example:

A I knew a cat who belonged to a little old lady who lived in a tiny cottage in the country. One day...

B **Sorry for interrupting, but** can you tell me more about the cottage, please?

A Well, it was very small - just three rooms. And it was thatched and there was a lovely garden in the front. **Anyway**, this cat once ran away...

C **Can I just ask,** what was the garden like?

A The garden? Well, it was full of flowers - it had even won a prize in a gardening competition. **But to get back to what I was saying,** the cat ran away...

D **Excuse me, but** I'd like to know more about the gardening competition.

Continue in this way for one or two minutes. Then another student starts talking about something.

1.3 Discussing stories

Listening to what others have to say is important in any discussion. You can help by encouraging people to contribute. Look at these phrases for bringing others into the discussion.

Don't you think so?
What do you think?
Right?
Don't you agree?
Do you know what I mean?
Are you with me?

Sit comfortably in a group of three or four and chat about your experiences of stories and story telling. Make sure everyone contributes to the discussion. Remember to use some of the phrases in the list above.

These questions may help your discussion:

1 What stories do you remember from your childhood?
2 Did your parents read aloud to you as a child? Do members of your family still read aloud to each other? Do you enjoy it? Why (not)?
3 Were you encouraged to read as a child? How old were you when you learned to read?
4 Has television killed story-telling?
5 Have you ever tried to write stories yourself?
6 What were/are some of your favourite stories?
7 If you are from different countries, did you nonetheless read similar fairy stories (e.g. *Cinderella*) when you were young?

1.4 Story telling

You are going to tell a story to other students in the class. It may be a folk tale from any part of the world, or a story you have read or been told by someone else - any story that you think your listeners will enjoy.

Rehearse the story at home and be prepared to tell it in class without using any notes.

Remember:

– Start with an expression or phrase to catch your listeners' attention.

– Vary your speed; use pauses to create drama or excitement.

– Use your voice to indicate different characters, to create atmosphere, to make the story more dramatic or exciting.

– When you reach the end of the story, make it clear that you are doing just that - from the language you use, from your voice or by any other appropriate means.

2.1 Shadow reading: a fairy story

Shadow read this story. (See **About this book - Shadow reading**, page 6 for instructions.)

Goldilocks and the Three Bears

Once upon a time there was a little girl called Goldilocks. She lived in a house at the edge of a big, dark wood. In the middle of the wood there was another house. Here there lived three bears: Father Bear, Mother Bear and tiny little Baby Bear.

Every morning Mother Bear cooked some porridge for breakfast. She put it into three bowls: a big bowl for Father Bear, a medium-sized bowl for Mother Bear and a teeny, weeny bowl for Baby Bear. One morning the porridge was rather hot, so the three bears went for a walk in the wood, while it cooled.

On that very morning Goldilocks was walking through the forest. She got lost. Suddenly she came to the little house where the three bears lived. The door was open. She peeped inside and, as no-one was there, she walked in. On the table she saw the three bowls of porridge. Goldilocks was hungry. She picked up Father Bear's big spoon and tasted the porridge in his big bowl. It was too hot! Then she tasted the porridge in the medium-sized bowl. It was too salty! Then she tasted the porridge in the tiny little bowl. It was just right! She ate it all up!

Then Goldilocks saw three chairs; a big chair, a medium-sized chair and a tiny little chair. She sat in the big chair. It was too high! She sat in the medium-sized chair. It was too hard! Then she sat in the tiny little chair. It was just right! But oh dear! The chair began to crack and then it broke. Goldilocks was too heavy for it.

Next, Goldilocks went upstairs to the bedroom, where there were three beds; a big bed, a medium-sized bed and a tiny little bed. She felt tired and so she climbed up onto the big bed. But it was too hard! Then she climbed up onto the medium-sized bed but that was too soft! Then Goldilocks lay down on the tiny little bed and it was just right! Soon she was fast asleep.

Soon the three bears came home. Father Bear looked at his big porridge bowl and said, 'Who's been eating *my* porridge?' Mother Bear looked at her medium-sized porridge bowl and said, 'Who's been eating *my* porridge?' Baby Bear looked at his tiny little porridge bowl and said, 'Who's been eating *my* porridge and eaten it all up?'

Then Father Bear looked at his big chair. 'Who's been sitting in *my* chair?' he asked. Then Mother Bear looked at her medium-sized chair. 'Who's been sitting in *my* chair?' Then Baby Bear looked at his tiny little chair. 'Who's been sitting in *my* chair and broken it?'

Next, the three bears went upstairs to the bedroom. Father Bear looked at his big bed. 'Who has been lying on *my* bed?' he asked. Mother Bear looked at her medium-sized bed. 'Who's been lying on *my* bed?' Baby Bear looked at his tiny little bed. 'Look who's lying in my bed!' he cried in his tiny voice. Goldilocks woke up and was so frightened when she saw the bears that she jumped out of the bed, ran down the stairs and out of the house. The three bears never saw her again.

2.2 Word study : sounds

With what do you associate the following sounds?

crack *creak* *crash* *crackle* *croak* *clink*
clap *click* *cluck* *clash* *clatter*

Practise saying each word thinking of the object, or whatever, that you associate with it. Try to make the way you enunciate consonants, the length you give to different vowels, and the pitch at which you say the word fit your association.

Repeat the exercise with these words:

snap *pop* *thump* *tick* *rattle* *hiss* *buzz*

2.3 Reading aloud : stories

Divide into two groups.

Group **A** will read the extract from **Three Men in a Boat** on page 84. Group **B** will read the extract from **Memories of Christmas** on page 91.

Practise reading aloud the text for your group. Discuss pausing, pace, emphasis, intonation, pronunciation and catenation with others in your group. (If the group is very large, divide into sub-groups, so that not more than three or four students are working together.) Read again the hints on reading aloud in **About this book – Reading aloud**, page 8.

Find a partner from the other group. Read your text aloud to your partner.

2.4 Interpreting : a visit to Scotland

This task is best done in a language laboratory.

Imagine you and a friend are planning a two-and-a-half-day trip to Edinburgh in Scotland. On the cassette you will hear a travel agent suggesting what you should do to get the most out of your short trip.

Your friend doesn't understand much English and so, as you listen to the travel agent, you interpret in your mother tongue what she is saying.

Remember that you are not translating, but *paraphrasing* what the travel agent is saying in order to allow your friend to understand all the main points.

The first time you do this exercise, you may want to give yourself a little more time by pausing the tape. Then do the exercise again pausing less - or not at all!

Rewind your tape and listen to your interpreting. What did you find difficult? Why?

Exchange booths with another student and compare each other's interpreting.

If you do this exercise with tape recorders in the classroom, see **About this book – Interpreting**, page 8 for some guidance.

unit 4

GOING SOLO

PART ONE

'Speaking' means communicating your thoughts to other people. Of course; simple. But the important word is 'your'. Not the thoughts of someone else, not ideas out of books or newspapers, but *your* thoughts. What *you* personally think about the subject.

C N MacKay, Speak for Yourself

1.1 Giving talks

Have you ever had to give a talk, in your own language or in English? What was the occasion? What was it about?

You are going to plan and prepare a five-minute talk to give to the rest of the class. The talk can be on any subject you wish, providing you can make it interest your audience. If you have time, you may be able to talk on a topic that will require some preliminary research. If you don't have much preparation time, you can use one of the suggestions given here.

Hobbies
The life story of someone you admire
A person you'd like to meet and why
Phobias
Capital punishment
The video boom
Soccer vandalism
Censorship
Euthanasia
Your favourite author
A journey you've been on
Your most embarrassing experience
Any other personal experience
How I became a (your profession)
Your job
An aspect of your job
If I had £5000...

Hints for preparing your talk

1 Write the topic of your talk in the middle of the page, e.g.

HOBBIES

2 Brain storm ideas, noting them down so that they radiate from the topic, e.g.

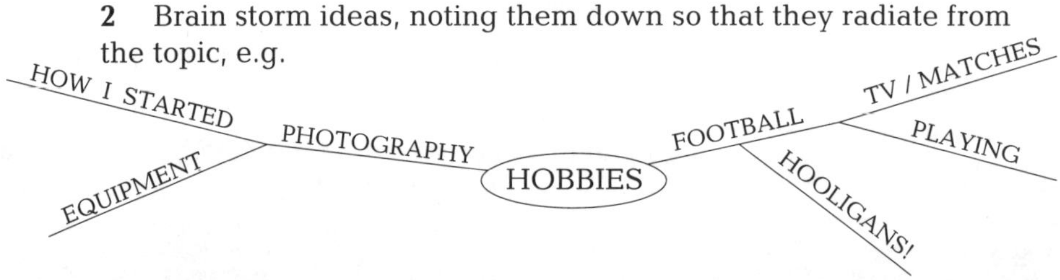

3 Sort out your ideas into an order for the talk, leaving out the ones you don't want.

4 Plan your talk so that:

- the topic is introduced (this should last about half a minute);
- the middle gives and develops all your important points (about four minutes). Use visual aids if this helps to put your points across (the blackboard, pictures, overhead projector transparencies);
- the conclusion either sums up your ideas (without just repeating them) or gives some kind of challenge to the audience. Whatever kind of ending you have, find some kind of high note to end on. Don't just say 'Well, that's all I have to say'!

Hints for giving your talk

Give your talk from the front of the class.

Use notes for reference, not for reading.

Look at your audience - you are talking to them and trying to interest them.

Speak clearly and audibly. Aim at those sitting furthest from you.

Be warm and friendly.

Be enthusiastic - to gain the audience's attention, and to hold it.

Don't give strings of facts - they are usually very hard to follow. Try to use vivid phrases.

Think of your body movements while you talk. Are you going to sit or stand? Are you going to walk around much? What are you going to do with your hands?

Feedback on your talk

Invite the class to ask you questions and to discuss some of the points you have raised.

In addition, by using the table on the next page, students can give you feedback on your talk and help you discover what your strengths and weaknesses are. If you record your talk (on audio or video), you can also use the table yourself.

Before the talk, discuss what the features mean.

During the talk students use the 5-point scale to comment on the features. (1 = very strong; 5 = weak - needs more practice.) Students may take different points, for example two people concentrating on audibility and voice quality, two on audience contact etc. They should also note down any comments they wish.

FEATURES	SCALE	COMMENTS
audibility and voice quality	1 2 3 4 5	
audience contact	1 2 3 4 5	
clarity of ideas and presentation	1 2 3 4 5	
interest of ideas and presentation	1 2 3 4 5	
fluency and ease of language	1 2 3 4 5	

1.2 Making a speech

1.2 Task 1

Work in small groups. Find out if anyone has ever had to give a formal speech, in English or in their mother tongue. What was the occasion? How did they feel before/during/after it?

When might you have to give a speech in the future?

Think of someone you have heard give a public speech either live or on TV or radio. What makes him/her a good speaker? Think about both content and delivery.

List some of the qualities that you think are needed by a good public speaker. Compare your list with other groups.

1.2 Task 2

Find words to complete these expressions. Then listen to the expressions on the cassette. Some of them may be different from yours. Discuss whether yours are also acceptable. Then listen and repeat the expressions.

Opening remarks

Good afternoon, ladies and ....

I'm .... to (*be with you this afternoon*).

It gives me great .... to (*introduce this afternoon's speaker*).

I'm .... today to (*tell you something of the work I have been doing*).

Summing up So, to .... I'd just like to say (*how much we have enjoyed the visit*).

In .... , ladies and gentlemen, (*I'd like to say – –*)

May I .... , once again, (*what a great pleasure it has been to be with you this afternoon*).

Thanking On .... of (*my colleagues*) I should like to thank (*the catering staff*) for (*looking after us so well*).

I should like to take this .... to say thank you to (*our speaker*).

I'm very .... for (*all that you have done for us*).

I am delighted to have been asked to .... a .... of thanks to (*all the staff*).

1.2 Task 3

Prepare and deliver a speech for:

either a situation in which you know you are likely to have to give a speech in English,

or one of the situations listed below. These situations are only described in outline. Use your imagination to supply any details you need.

None of the speeches should be long. One or two minutes is probably enough.

Remember that, when you are speaking on behalf of your fellow students/colleagues, you should look not only at the person your remarks are addressed to, but you should also return your glance to your colleagues. Turn back to the person you are addressing in your final thanks or your concluding remarks.

Situations

1 You are just coming to the end of a most enjoyable one-week residential holiday course in photography, held in Knighton, a small town in a beautiful part of Wales. You have been asked by the other students to give a speech on their behalf at the farewell dinner to thank all the staff (tutors and technicians, domestic staff, administrative staff).

Think about:

- why you enjoyed the course
- what you learned and why you value it
- any memorable moments during the course
- all the staff you should include in your thanks

2 You have been asked to introduce Mr Timothy Locke, who is coming to your college to give a lecture on *The British Monarchy: To be or not to be*. You have been given these notes about the speaker to help you prepare your short speech of introduction.

Timothy Locke, b. 15.11.39

1962 : BA in History and Economics (Univ. of London)
1965 : MA European History (Univ. of Sussex)
1966 - 73 : Lecturer in History, Brighton Polytechnic
1973 - 80 : Advisor on the EC, City of Brighton
1980 - : MP (Liberal) for Rockhill North

Publications include :
The British Monarchy 1901 - 1953, Wardington Press (1975)
Britain and the EC, Brighton Press (1980)

Hobbies : amateur dramatics, deep sea diving

Think about:

- what the speaker's qualifications are for dealing with the topic;
- why it is of interest to the audience.

Remember, your task is simply to bring the speaker and the audience together by creating an atmosphere of anticipation, sympathy and attention.

3 You are going with a group of people on a 2-hour tour around a factory/large department store/museum/exhibition. You will have to give a short speech of thanks on behalf of the group at the end of the tour.
Think about why it has been a useful/informative/enjoyable tour.

4 You will be a guest of honour at a formal dinner to which many important people who work in your field have been invited. You know that you will be given a farewell gift, at which point you will have to give a speech of thanks.

Include an expression of your thanks and a brief tribute or expression of your appreciation to the group of people who are represented at the dinner.

1.3 A game : Just a Minute

This activity is based on a radio programme of the same name, which is broadcast on BBC Radio 4 and on the BBC World Service. Two versions are given here. Choose which you want to do.

Version 1

The teacher or chairperson announces a topic, e.g. Money / My favourite things / Holidays. The chairperson counts from 1 to 5, to give the first player a little time to think. The first player then tries to talk for one minute on the topic *without repeating any content words* i.e. nouns, adjectives, adverbs, verbs (except *to be, to have* and modals). If the player is successful, he or she gains two points.

If any other player notices a repetition, they call 'Stop' and say which word was repeated. This player then continues talking, trying to complete the minute, either talking about the same topic, or moving to an associated topic using a phrase like 'Talking of .... / That reminds me of ....' The player who is talking when the minute is up gains one point.

The chairperson will need a stop-watch to count the minute, stopping it while repetitions are discussed.

Version 2

Again, the teacher can announce a topic. Alternatively, on separate bits of paper, students write four or five topics (preferably of one word each). Put all the bits of paper into an envelope or plastic bag.

The first player takes a paper from the bag. The chairperson counts from 1 to 5. The first player then tries to talk for one minute on the topic indicated on the paper *without making a mistake in grammar or vocabulary*. If the player is successful, he or she gains two points. Any player who hears a mistake calls 'Stop'. If it is an incorrect challenge (i.e. there is no mistake), the speaker gains a point and continues talking. If there is a mistake and the challenger can correct it, the challenger gains a point and continues talking about the same subject; if the challenger cannot correct the mistake but someone else can, the challenger does not gain a point but does continue talking about the subject. This player can be similarly challenged by anyone who hears, or thinks they hear, a mistake – and so on. The player who is talking when the minute ends gains one point.

PART TWO

2.1 Shadow reading : enunciation and projection

Shadow read these texts.

1 The Modern Major General

In Britain Gilbert and Sullivan are a much-loved partnership who collaborated in writing the libretto and the music for a series of comic operas. This song is taken from *The Pirates of Penzance*.

As you shadow read it, make sure that you enunciate every consonant clearly.

I am the very model of a modern Major-General,
I've information vegetable, animal and mineral.
I know the Kings of England and I quote the fights historical;
From Marathon to Waterloo, in order categorical;
I'm very well acquainted too with matters mathematical,
I understand equations either simple or quadratical,
About binomial theorem I'm teeming with a lot o' news -
With many cheerful facts about the square of the hypotenuse.
I'm very good at integral and differential calculus,
I know the scientific names of beings animalculus;
In short, in matters vegetable, animal and mineral,
I am the very model of a modern Major-General.

2 Introducing the speaker

Gussie Fink-Nottle has been asked to give a speech at a school prize-giving ceremony. The headmaster introduces him to the audience.

'Today' said the bearded bloke, 'we are all happy to welcome as the guest of the afternoon Mr Fitz-Wattle...'
Gussie sat up with a jerk.
'Fink-Nottle', he said opening his eyes.
'Fitz-Nottle.'

'Fink-Nottle.'

'I should say Fink-Nottle.'

'Of course you should, you silly ass,' said Gussie genially. 'All right, get on with it.'

'We are all happy, I say, to welcome as the guest of the afternoon Mr Fink-Nottle, who has kindly consented to award the prizes. This task, as you know, is one that should have devolved upon that well-beloved and vigorous member of our board of governors, the Rev. William Plomer, and we are all, I am sure, very sorry that illness at the last moment should have prevented him from being here today. But, if I may borrow a familiar metaphor from the - if I may employ a homely metaphor familiar to you all - what we lost on the swings we gain on the roundabouts.'

He paused and beamed rather freely, to show that this was comedy. I could have told the man it was no use. Not a ripple.

It's always a nasty jar to wait for the laugh and find that the gag hasn't got across. The bearded bloke was visibly discomposed. At that, however, I think he would have got by, had he not, at this juncture, unfortunately stirred Gussie up again.

'In other words, though deprived of Mr Plomer, we have with us this afternoon Mr Fink-Nottle. I am sure that Mr Fink-Nottle's name is one that needs no introduction to you. It is, I venture to assert, a name that is familiar to us all.'

'Not to you,' said Gussie.

And the next moment I saw what Jeeves had meant when he had described Gussie as laughting heartily. 'Heartily' was absolutely the 'mot juste'. It sounded like a gas explosion,.

'You didn't seem to know it so dashed well, what?' said

Gussie. And, reminded apparently by the word 'what' of the word 'Wattle', he repeated the latter some sixteen times with a rising inflection.
'Wattle, Wattle, Wattle,' he concluded. 'Right-ho. Push on.'

2.2 Word study : clichés

Introducing the speaker includes several clichés, e.g.

– 'We are all happy to welcome ...'
– 'What we lost on the swings we gain on the roundabouts'

Can you find any others?

Where did you meet clichés in Part 1 of this unit?
Listen to the conversation below. Then work in pairs. The writer makes fun of clichés used in everyday speech. Discuss the meaning of the clichés and suggest alternative language.

Eric is in a bar having a drink. His friend Derek comes in.

Derek	I say, Eric *old man, long time no see.*
Eric	Ah, Derek! Care to join me? *What's your poison?*
Derek	Well, *since you twist my arm...!*
Eric	*What'll it be* then?
Derek	*Spot of the old vino*, if you don't mind.
Eric	*Prefer the grape to the grain*, eh?
Derek	Got to watch the *old ticker*.
Eric	(confidentially) I'll just *summon a lackey*...*Mine host*! A glass of the *vino tinto* for the *walking wounded*.

(Mine host goes about his business.)

Derek	How's the *lovely lady wife?*
Eric	The *better half? Positively blooming.* Mind you, spends far too much time at home watching the *one-eyed God* and smoking *coffin nails.* (Pause) I had a very nasty experience at the weekend, Derek. (Mine host appears with the vino tinto.) *What's the damage?*
Mine host	One pound ten.
Eric	There you are. Anyway, there I was, *beetling along*, foot on the *loud pedal*, when one of *our two-wheeled chums* came off a roundabout *like a bat out of hell.* All of a sudden it *looked like curtains* for *yours truly.*
Derek	You thought, *'This is it!'*
Eric	And how! *Slammed on the anchor,* I did - and just missed *chummy* by a *coat of paint.* I'd nearly *run out of road.* Fortunately the *boys in blue* weren't in sight. So I *gave him an earful.* Told him he ought to *exercise the little grey cells a mite more often.* And left it at that.

2.3 Reading aloud : speeches

Read this text aloud. (See hints for reading aloud in **About this book**, page 8.)

Speeches

Just a few words. Yes, but which? Why did I agree to go to the dinner in the first place? I shan't be able to eat or drink. Dare I leave it to the spur of the moment? Chuck it in at the last minute? Simply send a greetings telegram apologizing for a head cold? How long do they expect me to go on, and about what for heaven's sake? What sort of idiots are they who are willing to pay seven guineas for a ticket? At least they won't expect me to pay, or will they? Of course not, I am singing for my supper.

"I realize that to sing for one's supper demands a voice truer than my own. But I felt I simply had to come here this evening to propose the toast of the guests and particularly Mrs Blenkinsop, the well-known ex-prison governor." (That's what they say she did.) "I only hope there won't be a riot here this evening." That would put the cat among the pigeons. Cat among the pigeons? "I feel like a cat among ..." or better, perhaps, "We all feel we are pigeons flocking to welcome the cat." Hopeless. Better to leave Mrs B out altogether than insult the poor woman. How about, "Ladies and Gentlemen, my brief is to introduce our guests, handcuffed to the name of the principal speaker Mrs Blenkinsop." People don't like long speeches. "Mrs Blenkinsop must by this time be used to captive audiences but I suggest to you that this is the first time..." for what in heaven's name? Concentrate. How long have I got? Where's the calendar? Another month?

There must be more important things to worry about; it's just that at this moment I can't think of them.

2.4 Interpreting : at the British Museum

This task is best done in a language laboratory.

On the cassette you can hear John Reeve, who works at the British Museum in London. He explains how the ancient Egyptians mummified their dead.

Imagine that you are at the Museum with a friend who doesn't understand English. While John Reeve is talking, try to interpret what he is saying to your friend.

Remember that you are not translating, but *paraphrasing* what John Reeve is saying in order to allow your friend to understand all the main points.

The first time you do the exercise, you may want to give yourself a little more time by pausing the tape. Then do the exercise again pausing less - or not at all!

Rewind your tape and listen to your interpreting. What did you find difficult? Why?

Exchange booths with another student and compare each other's interpreting.

If you do this exercise with tape recorders in the classroom, see **About this book - Interpreting**, page 8 for some guidance.

unit 5

DEBATING

PART ONE

Advice on debating : Keep alert. Have paper and pencil for reminder notes; keep calm; be good-tempered and occasionally humorous; be sincere but not too intense. Give yourself pauses in which to reflect, to be received, to emphasise and relax. Make eye-ball to eye-ball contact with your listeners. Don't read, talk. Make a few firm convincing points rather than a number of weak ones and try to have a forceful word at the end of each statement.

C Burniston and J Parry, Direct Speech

In this unit you are going to prepare for and take part in a formal debate.

1.1 What is a debate?

1.1 Task 1

Read this description of a debate.

> A debate is a formal, organised argument. It revolves around a *motion*, usually given in the affirmative, on which a *vote* is taken.
>
> The debate is organised by *time* and by a *set of procedures*. It is conducted by a *chairperson* (*the Chair*).
>
> Two opposing parties try to convince a third party (the audience) that each party's argument has more merit than the other. The *affirmative team* asks the audience to accept the motion; the *negative team* asks the audience to reject it. At the end of the debate the audience *votes* for or against the motion.
>
> The affirmative team consists of a *proposer* and a *seconder*. The negative team consists of an *opposer* and a *seconder*.

Work in small groups. Draw a plan of your classroom showing how you could arrange a debate in it. Compare your plan with other groups. Decide which arrangement you will use.

1.1 Task 2

The language used in a debate is always very formal.

Look at these expressions. Choose the one in each pair which you think is most appropriate for use in a debate. Then listen to the cassette, where you can hear the most appropriate expressions.

1 The Chair says:
   a) The subject we're going to debate today is 'The present prison system should be abolished.'
   b) The motion before the house today is 'This house believes that the present prison system should be abolished.'

2 The Chair says:
   a) This is Maria and this is Peter. They are going to try and persuade you that the motion is right/wrong.
   b) I'd like to introduce you to the team which is going to speak in favour of the motion/to oppose the motion. Their names are Miss Maria Gomez and Mr Peter von Mark.

3 The Chair says:
   a) I would now like to call on Miss Maria Gomez to present the case for the motion.
   b) Maria, it's your turn to speak for the motion.

4 The Proposer says:
   a) Before presenting my arguments in favour of the motion, I would like to present important background information.
   b) Do any of you know the background to this topic? Okay, in case you don't, I'll tell you.

5 The Chair says:
   a) Would anyone in the audience like to ask a question?
   b) The debate is now open to the floor.

6 A member of the audience says:
   a) The first speaker said ....
   b) Maria said ....

7 A member of the audience says:
   a) Maria, could you please tell my why ....
   b) Mr Chairman/Madam Chair, I would like to ask the first speaker why....

8 The Chair says:
   a) I call on the audience to behave in an orderly manner.
   b) Please be quiet.

9 The Chair says:
   a) Please put up your hands if you are voting for/against the motion.
   b) Would members of the audience please raise their hands if they are voting in favour of/against the motion.

10 The Chair says:
   a) The majority of the audience have voted in favour of the motion/against the motion.
   b) I declare that the motion has been carried/defeated.

1.1 Task 3

When a motion is first suggested for debate, it is important that all terms in it are carefully defined by both sides. If this is not done, the debate can become pointless because the two teams have a different understanding of the key terms.

Work in groups of four or five. Imagine the motion 'The private life of a public figure should affect his eligibility for office' has been suggested for debate. Can you agree on one interpretation for:

1 *private life*

Private life refers to:
a) the marital relationship between the candidate and spouse
b) the occupation of the spouse
c) the relationship between the candidate and the offspring
d) the occupations of the offspring
e) the social connections of the candidate
f) all of the above

2 *a public figure*

A public figure refers to:
a) a politician
b) an entertainment star
c) a performing artist
d) a doctor
e) anybody whose name is well known to the public

If you cannot agree within five minutes on acceptable interpretations of both these terms, then the topic is not suitable for a debate.

1.1 Task 4

In groups, examine these motions carefully. Which ones are suitable for debate, i.e. in which ones can all terms be satisfactorily defined?

1. Corporal punishment is necessary in schools.
2. Nuclear weapons should be destroyed.
3. The possession of marijuana should be legalised.
4. Women have equal opportunities (in our country/in Britain).
5. Prisons should be abolished.
6. Euthanasia should be legalised.
7. Advertisers perform a useful service to the community.
8. Young people should have the vote at (16).
9. A year of community service should be obligatory between the ages of 16 and 20.
10. Women should dress to please men.

1.1 Task 5

Between them, the speeches of the proposer, the opposer and the seconders must include:

1 *Background information.* This is usually offered by the proposer, but it can be challenged by the opposition.

2 *Needs arguments*, to demonstrate the need/lack of need to change the status quo (the existing state of affairs).

3 *Rebuttal* – proof that the arguments presented by the other team are false. It is the responsibility of the seconders of each team to rebut the arguments of the proposer and opposer.

4 *A sum-up*. This should be a short statement which clinches the case. Each team has the opportunity to sum up. The team decides which member will undertake this.

A popular British magazine, *Living*, used to publish a written form of debate with one statement *for* and one *against* the motion. Readers were invited to vote on the motion. Here is the case presented by the Earl of Longford for the motion 'The present prison system should be abolished'.

Read the text.
Does it include any background information?
Does it sum up the case?
What rebuttal(s) does the Earl of Longford make, predicting arguments that he thinks will be made by the opposition?

'The present prison system should be abolished'

FOR
The Earl of Longford, former leader of the House of Lords and penal reformer

The present prison system is full of disgraceful features and in a truly civilised society wouldn't be tolerated for a moment. Short sentences are bad for inmates because the short-term prisons are so grossly over-crowded, and long-term prisoners are damaged by the length of the sentence.

We're locking far too many people up for far too long. In Britain we use prison more freely and pass much longer sentences than in any other European country.

Of course we have to maintain law and order, but recent research has shown that heavy sentences don't act as a deterrent, and that the longer you spend in prison the more likely it is to leave you embittered.

Violent criminals are frequently mentally disturbed people and should be cared for in hospital. Sane people hardly ever kill more than once. Of course there's always got to be some risk when finally freeing people who've been violent, but we've got to take that risk out of sheer humanity. It's all very well saying think of the victim - I have proved that I do - but you can't allow victims' or their relatives' hatred to affect justice.

Prison is especially bad for young people. It's wicked to inflict it on those who are in any way disturbed, and the tough ones take a pride in going through it. It's the greatest possible mistake to give them the idea early on in life that they're criminals.

Furthermore, prison is very uneconomic. It is many times cheaper to give someone a sentence of community service than it is to send him/her to gaol. The right alternatives already exist but are not being sufficiently used. Instead of building new prisons we should double the number of probation officers, so that more people could be cared for within the community.

1.1 Task 6

In any debate, it is important for both speakers and audience to be aware that some arguments are based on *opinion* and some on *objective evidence*.

Read the text again and identify the arguments given. Which ones are based on opinion? Which ones are, or seem to be, based on objective evidence?

Look at the rebuttals that you identified in Task 5. Do you think that the strategy of rebutting before presenting a *needs argument* is a good one?

1.1 Task 7

List as many arguements as you can think of opposing the motion in Task 5. For which of your arguments could you find objective evidence to strengthen your claims? What *sources* would you need to locate to find this evidence?

1.1 Task 8

Choose one of the motions in Task 4 that you decided could be used for a debate.

What background would need to be given in the debate? Where would you find sources for objective evidence?

Divide into pairs. Write down as many *needs arguments* as you can, both for and against the motion.

Pool your arguments with the rest of the class. Is the class able collectively to come up with good arguments for both sides?

1.2 Preparing a debate

1.2 Task 1

Work in groups of four. Each group should choose a different motion for debate.

Define the terms of the motion.

Decide who is going to be the team proposing the motion and who is the team opposing it. (Notice that you do not need to choose according to your conviction - in fact, it can be more interesting for you to argue a point of view you do not actually hold.)

The two teams will now prepare their presentations independently of each other. Each of the four speakers will have five minutes in which to speak.

Both teams should:

- consider the background to the motion (even though it will be for the proposer of the motion to present this in the debate);
- remember that the essence of debate is finding holes in your opponents' arguments and finding ways of showing that these holes exist;
- predict the arguments that the other team will come up with and be ready with rebuttals;
- decide on your strategy, e.g. will you rebut arguments before or after they are offered?
- plan how to divide what you want to say between the proposer/opposer and the seconder.

You may use any sources (books, etc.) you wish and bring these with you to the debate.

1.3 The debate

Procedure

The debate is conducted by the Chair. The Chair is responsible for the smooth running of the debate. The Chair is also responsible for making on-the-spot decisions about any unpredicted problems that arise during the debate.

The Chair:

1 announces the motion for debate, introduces the speakers to the audience and explains the procedure.

2 asks the team proposing the motion to define the terms in the motion. The opposing team are asked whether they accept these definitions.

3 tells the speakers that they will each have five minutes in which to present their case and that the Chair will warn them when the five minutes are almost up by passing them a message on a piece of paper. The speakers are invited to speak in the following order:

   - the proposer of the motion
   - the opposer of the motion
   - the seconder for the motion
   - the seconder against the motion.

4 invites questions from the floor (reminding them that the questions must be put through the Chair), setting a time-limit of five minutes.

5 invites each team to sum up its arguments. (This should be a quick summary of the arguments which the other side has not successfully countered.)

6 asks the floor to vote for or against the motion.

7 counts the votes.

8 declares the motion carried or defeated.

Voting

The members of the audience should vote *according to their assessment of each team's performance*, rather than their personal attitude to the motion. They should use copies of this table to make their assessment of each speaker. Each feature should be rated from 1 to 5 where 1 = very poor and 5 = excellent.

persuasiveness, including sincerity and conviction with which speech is delivered	1 2 3 4 5
imaginativeness of arguments	1 2 3 4 5
language competence	1 2 3 4 5
attitude towards debate	1 2 3 4 5

If the vote is equal for and against the motion, the Chair has the casting vote.

Timing

The whole debate should last about forty to forty-five minutes. This allows the speakers five minutes for each speech; five minutes for questions from the floor; about ten minutes for procedural matters including the final vote.

After the debate

When the debate is over, the speakers may like to state their true position regarding the motion. Members of the audience may like to say whether their opinion was changed by the speakers' arguments. The evaluations of each speaker may also be discussed.

PART TWO

2.1 Shadow reading : debaters and persuaders

Shadow read these texts. (See **About this book - Shadow reading**, page 6 for instructions.)

1 Hamlet Act 3, Scene 1 – Shakespeare

To be, or not to be - that is the question;
Whether 'tis nobler in the mind to suffer
The slings and arrows of outrageous fortune,
Or to take arms against a sea of troubles,
And by opposing end them? To die, to sleep –
No more; and by a sleep to say we end
The heart-ache and the thousand natural shocks
That flesh is heir to. 'Tis a consummmation
Devoutly to be wish'd. To die, to sleep;
To sleep, perchance to dream. Ay, there's the rub;
For in that sleep of death what dreams may come,
When we have shuffled off this mortal coil,
Must give us pause.

2 Why twenty-one?

Although this text is from a written article, it could very well be part of a formal opening speech in a debate on the motion: 'Young people should have the vote at eighteen'. It was written before the law was changed in Britain lowering the minimum voting age from twenty-one to eighteen and before the abolition of capital punishment.

I am led to wonder why in England and in many other countries of the West the twenty-first birthday forms the frontier between legal infancy and responsibility. Why should the number twenty-one possess a significance so mystical? Is it because twenty-one is a multiple of that occult number seven? Is it because it represents a generation plus one year? Enquiries of eminent legal authorities have been met only with embarrassed ignorance.

It seems mad enough that from the age of eighteen onwards boys can swing for the murder of a policeman, but are still not entitled to vote or to be sued in the courts for debt.

In France, before the Revolution, the Kings attained their majority, I fancy, at the age of fifteen - Louis XV, if I remember rightly, celebrated his fifteenth birthday by ending the regency of the duc de Bourbon under which he had increasingly chafed; and the luckless Kings of the Arab world - where the assassin's bomb or bullet lifts babies to the throne more often than not - also, I believe, regard fifteen as the natural age when regal powers are assumed.

During the recent General Election, the Labour Party suggested that the qualifying age for voters should be lowered below twenty-one to eighteen.

There is in theory at least a strong case for intelligence tests before a citizen is entitled to cast a vote. There might also be something to be said for raising the minimum voting age to twenty-five or even thirty. But if you accept the assumption that anyone of twenty-one is fit to decide how the country shall be governed, then, why not eighteen? If by that age a young creature has not got his wits about him, he never will.

2.2 Word study : politics and elections

2.2 Task 1

All the words and phrases at the top of the next page belong to the same lexical area of politics and elections. Use dictionaries and lexicons to check the meaning of any words that are unfamiliar.

vote (v. and n.)	*a candidate*
to cast a vote	*to nominate*
poll (v. and n.)	*to stand for (election/parliament)*
polling booth	*to canvass*
polling day	*manifesto*
polling station	*campaign* (v. and n.)
ballot paper	*constituency*
(general) election	*proportional representation*
electorate	
electoral roll/register	

Are there any words you think should be added to this list?

2.2 Task 2

Prepare a short talk to explain the electoral system in your country or in any other country you like.

2.3 Reading aloud : the Gettysburg Address

This speech was made by Abraham Lincoln, in November 1863 during the American Civil War, to consecrate the battlefield at Gettysburg as a national cemetery.

Prepare to read the speech aloud by marking pauses, catenation, intonation, etc. Think carefully about how you can highlight certain key words, and experiment in changing the main word stress in some sense groups. For example:

> *'Four <u>score</u> and seven years ago ....'*
> *'Four score and <u>seven</u> years ago ....'*

Think also about the speed at which you are going to read aloud.

Read again the hints on reading aloud in **About this book - Reading aloud**, page 8.

> " Four score and seven years ago our fathers brought forth on this continent a new nation, conceived in liberty, and dedicated to the proposition that all men are created equal. Now we are engaged in a great civil war, testing whether that nation, or any nation so conceived and so dedicated, can long endure. We are met on a great battlefield of that war. We have come to dedicate a portion of that field as a

final resting-place for those who here gave their lives that the nation might live. It is altogether fitting and proper that we should do this. But, in a larger sense, we cannot dedicate - we cannot consecrate - we cannot hallow - this ground. The brave men, living and dead, who struggled here have consecrated it, far above our poor power to add or detract. It is rather for us to be here dedicated to the great task remaining before us - that from these honoured dead we take increased devotion to that cause for which they have the last full measure of devotion - that we here highly resolve that these dead shall not have died in vain - that this nation, under God, shall have a new birth of freedom and that government of the people, by the people, for the people, shall not perish from the earth. ”

2.4 *Interpreting : summarising from the newspaper*

Work in pairs. Each of you should read a newspaper or magazine in your own language. Find some news items that you think will interest your partner. Summarise them orally in English for your partner. (Remember : don't translate the items. Your summary should be about two thirds the length of the original news item.)

unit 6

NEGOTIATING TALK

PART ONE

Talking is a kind of tactical manoeuvring.

H Widdowson, Teaching Language as Communication

1.1 Clarifying points

Look at these phrases:

A *So what | you're / he's | saying / getting at / trying to | say / get at | is...*

If I understand | you / him | right, | you feel/think ... / he feels/thinks ....

You mean / He means | ....

B *Yes, that's right.*

Exactly.

No, not quite.

No, that's not quite what | I mean. / he means.

No, I don't think that's quite what he means.

No, | I'm / he's | not saying that at all.

Work in pairs. Look at these quotations. Clarify what you think the author meant, using phrases from the list above.

1 'Ask not what your country will do for you - ask what you can do for your country.' (J F Kennedy: Presidential inaugural address, 1961)

2 'It's the criminal classes that keep the police off the dole.' (Graffiti on London subway.)

3 'It is when I am struggling to be brief that I become unintelligible.' (Horace)

4 'Be wise in time and turn your horse out to grass when he shows signs of age, lest he end in a ludicrous breakdown with straining flanks.' (Horace)

5 'He who has begun his task has half done it.' (Horace)

6 'We are never knowingly undersold.' (Shop slogan : John Lewis partnership)

7 'Politicians are the same all over. They promise to build a bridge even when there's no river.' (N. Krushchev : Comment to reporters in the USA, October 1960)

8 'I wouldn't say when you've seen one Western you've seen the lot; but when you've seen the lot you get the feeling you've seen one.' (Katherine Whitehorn : *Decoding the West* in 'Sunday Best')

9 'Marriage is a bribe to make a housekeeper think she's a householder.' (Thornton Wilder : *The Matchmaker*)

10 'Television is a form of soliloquy.' (Kenneth Clark, *The Guardian* 26.11.77)

11 'She's leaving home after living alone for so many years.' (John Lennon and Paul McCartney, *She's leaving home*)

1.2 Thinking about discussion

1.2 Task 1

Work in groups of six or seven. Two of you will be observers while the others have a discussion for about five to seven minutes, either on a topic of their choice or on one of the topics listed at the end of Task 2.

During the discussion the observers will make notes on ways in which the speakers negotiate and communicate with each other.

Observer **A** will make notes on the language the speakers use to:

- encourage each other to continue speaking (E)
- redirect the discussion (RD)
- return to a previous topic (RT)

Observer **B** will make notes on the language the speakers use to:

- bring others into the discussion (BI)
- ask for and offer clarification (C)
- interrupt or break into the discussion (I)

To make the observation sheet, draw one large square for each speaker on a piece of paper. Make your notes in the boxes. Use the code letters and write down as much as you can of the language used.

At the end of the discussion, the whole group should discuss the observers' notes.

An observation sheet for a discussion with four people could look something like this

ISABEL	YUKI
E - Really! C - You mean ... I - Excuse me ... BI - What do you think, Yuki?	E - That's true RD - That reminds me of ... E - Goodness! E - How interesting. E - I hadn't thought of that.
JAN	**PETER**
RT - To go back to what you were saying before about ... E - (repeats what Peter said)	E - last week? Really? E - I see. Yes ... C - No, that's not quite what I mean. I mean ... I - I'm sorry to interrupt you Isabel, but ...

1.2 Task 2

At different times and with different people we discuss a topic in different ways and for different purposes. For example we may be trying to:

- clarify our thinking by putting it into words
- explore the meaning of something with others
- find out someone else's opinion or ideas
- bring others over to our point of view
- have a good argument
- avoid talking about some aspects of the topic

Would you like to add to this list?

Think back on the discussion you have just had. What was your purpose? How did it affect things like:

- encouraging others to continue talking?
- redirecting the discussion?
- bringing others into the discussion?
- clarifying points?
- agreeing and disagreeing?
- interrupting?

Have another discussion on a different topic. Choose new observers and proceed as in Task 1.

Suggested topics for discussion

1 Is there a case for censorship of the media?
2 Do we give enough help to the physically handicapped?
3 Protest demonstrations are a waste of time.
4 The superpowers spend too much on space exploration.
5 Sex stereotyping starts at birth.
6 The only thing people are interested in today is earning more money.
7 Examinations exert a very bad influence on education.
8 Parents are too permissive with their children.

1.3 A chatathon

You are going to take part in a competition to find out who is the best conversationalist in the class.

Procedure

Stage 1 : 15-minute conversations (all students)

Stage 1 consists of a series of 15-minute conversations in pairs, with short breaks between each conversation.

1 Before the beginning of each conversation the controller will put you into threes. Two of you will be conversationalists and converse with each other. The third will judge the conversation. You will be in a different group for each conversation. Everyone should be a conversationalist in at least three conversations.

2 There will be one topic of conversation for each 15-minute conversation. This will be announced by the Controller. As soon as the topic has been announced, the conversationalists should begin.

3 The conversationalists must keep conversing throughout the session. They should keep to the topic throughout the conversation. They are not allowed to make notes.

4 The judges should sit where they can see the two conversationalists but where their presence is as unobtrusive as possible. The judges only listen and do not take any part in the conversations.

5 At the end of the conversation the judge will award points out of 20 to each conversationalist (see *Guidelines for judges* on the next page). The judge may penalise conversationalists for pauses, monologues, rudeness, unintelligibility. Laughter is not penalised unless it is unduly long.

6 The judges' opinions are final. At the end of each conversation, the judges will give the Controller a note of the marks they have awarded, like this:

```
Stage 1 : Conversation no. .....   Judge ..........

Conversationalists          Marks

....................        ............

....................        ............
```

The Controller will reveal the scores only at the end of Stage 1.

The four highest scoring conversationalists will proceed to the semi-finals in Stage 2. (If not everybody has taken part in the same number of conversations, all scores will be averaged.)

Stage 2 : Semi-final (4 students)

1 The semi-final consists of one conversation per pair, lasting twenty minutes.

2 The topic of conversation will be announced by the Controller and the conversationalists will begin conversing immediately.

3 Each pair will have three judges, allocated by the Controller.

4 The scores from Stage 1 will not be taken into account in deciding upon the winners of the semi-final.

5 The judges need only decide which of their pair is best. They do not need to give a score.

6 The winner from each pair will proceed to the Final in Stage 3.

7 In all other respects, the rules are the same as for Stage 1.

Stage 3 : The Final (2 students)

1 The Final will be one conversation lasting twenty minutes.

2 The conversation will be judged by the rest of the students in the class, who will choose the winner through a secret ballot at the end of the conversation.

3 In all other respects, the rules are the same as for Stage 1.

Guidelines for judges

1 You should avoid taking part in the conversation or giving any reaction to what the conversationalists are saying.

2 Try to avoid making any notes during the conversation, for this can affect the conversationalists' concentration.

3 It is possible for both conversationalists to be awarded the same score. Your score will be based on your overall impression of each conversationalist. However you should take the following matters into consideration:

Style How do the conversationalists converse? Think about these points:

Positive	*Negative*
Listening	Interrupting/blocking
Responsiveness	Lecturing/monologue
	Interview
Flow/fluency	Pausing
Cogency	Repetition
Apt use of physical gesture	Repeated verbal/physical mannerisms
Humour	Dullness
Clarity	Unintelligibility
Accurate use of language	Inaccurate use of language
Imaginative use of language/ wide vocabulary range	Limited range of vocabulary/ sentence patterns
Courtesy	Rudeness/quarrelling/swearing

Content How do the conversationalists deal with the topic of conversation?

1 Lucid, logical and perceptive exploration of the topic (while keeping within its bounds).

2 Selection, clarity and effectiveness of ideas.

2.1 Shadow reading : 'You, wife - me, pop star'

Shadow read this text. (See **About this book - Shadow reading**, page 6 for instructions.)

You, wife - me, pop star

I have lately been contemplating the up and down life of a 'just pop' man. I do not mean Elvis, Tom or Englebert, who don't sing opera, just pop. I mean me and all the other victims of 'Just pop the kettle on...' 'Just pop upstairs ...' 'Just pop down to the bread shop ...' and all the other 'just pop' tricks.

'Just pop' is closely related to the 'While you're on your feet...' trap and 'Before you sit down...' and should always be viewed with extreme caution. Wives, mothers - indeed the whole of the female species - are great users of it.

I've been 'just popping' ever since I was a lad, and my marriage has been popping along for years, with me the pop star. Here a pop, there a pop, everywhere a pop-pop.

The very words 'just pop...' are designed, of course, to diminish any task in the eyes, or rather ears, of all right-thinking people, thus making protest impossible, or at the least churlish. This is the first law of 'just pop...'

The second law is that the tone of voice accompanying the request is also pitched a semi-octave lower, a low murmur in fact, and delivered in a throw-away, deprecating manner to fool the 'poppee' into further complacency about the task before him. In this way he can finish up doing no end of dreary jobs.

(Errands and tasks that started out with a smile and a casual 'Just pop...' have involved me in miles of walking, hours of toil and untold expense, of which I, the naive 'poppee', had no hint.)

Only the other day I was jolted to hear the words slipping easily off the lips of one small daughter. 'If you're going out, daddy, would you just pop into the library and get me a couple of books on Paris? We're doing a project.' The library was a mile out of my way and books on Paris in the geographical section were like needles in a haystack.

2.2 *Word study : ups and downs and ins and outs*

2.2 Task 1

What is meant by *an up and down life...?* (See lines 1-2 of the Shadow Reading text on page 73.)

Look at the examples below. Explain the meaning of each phrase in italics. Use a dictionary if necessary.

1 The company I work for is *on the up and up*.

2 I feel my life has been full of *ups and downs*, but on the whole there have been more *ups* than *downs*.

3 The room was in a terrible mess - the thieves had turned it completely *upside down*.

4 All the *down and outs* of the town live under the railway bridge.

5 I can't understand all the *ins and outs* of this computer system.

6 My friend knows that computer system *inside out*. She'll be able to help you.

7 They say it brings good luck to put your clothes on *inside out* or *back to front* - as long as you don't notice what you've done till the end of the day!

8 Don't listen to him. He's an *out-and-out* liar.

2.2 Task 2

Use a good English-English dictionary to explore the words *up, down, in, out, inside, outside, back, front.*

Share with other students any meanings and expressions that you found particularly interesting.

2.3 *Reading aloud : letters*

2.3 Task 1

This ad was placed in the 'Lonely Hearts' column of the weekly British magazine *Private Eye*:

Attractive Petite Blonde female, 27, working in London, enjoys cinema, theatre, classical music and jazz, would like to hear from intelligent stimulating men. View to romantic but lasting relationship. Box 000.

Work in threes. Imagine you are friends of Annette, the girl who placed the ad. You are each going to read aloud one of the replies that Annette received. Which one seems the most interesting? Why?

A will read letter **A** on page 85.
B will read letter **B** on page 88.
C will read letter **C** on page 92.

(For hints on reading aloud, see **About this book - Reading aloud** page 8.)

2.3 Task 2

Do you find 'Lonely Hearts' advertisements in your country? Would you expect replies like those you have read, or are there significant cultural differences which would affect the way people would respond?

Do you know anyone who has used 'Lonely Hearts' advertisements?

Do you think such advertisements serve a useful social purpose?

2.4 Interpreting : radio and TV news

2.4 Task 1

Work in pairs. You must both share a language other than English.

You are going to listen to a recording of a TV or radio news bulletin in English.

A is a guest in **B**'s home. **A** speaks practically no English. **B** therefore has to interpret the gist of the news while you are both listening to it. (In other words, **B** must interpret without pausing the tape.)

After two or three news items, swop roles, so that **A** is interpreting for **B**.

2.4 Task 2

Listen to the news bulletin again, but this time pause the tape at the end of each item. Give a fuller interpretation of each item.

2.4 Task 3

Repeat Tasks 1 and 2, but this time listen to a news bulletin in your mother tongue for interpretation into English.

KEEPING UP YOUR ENGLISH

How can you keep up your spoken English when you are no longer attending a course? It is important to take time to think about this carefully.

1 Keeping up your English at home

Task 1

Take five minutes to write down as many ways as you can think of for keeping up your English. Exchange your ideas with the rest of the class. Make a note of the ones you think are most useful and practical.

Task 2

Read through this list of strategies. Are there any new ones that you hadn't thought of before? Discuss them with other students. Which ones do you think are interesting and useful?

1 Record yourself reading aloud. Listen carefully to your pronunciation, intonation, stress, rhythm, pace, pitch etc.

2 Try to get hold of speech recordings, for example plays, novels, and poetry read aloud and recorded on cassette. Use them for 'listen and repeat' practice and for shadow reading.
(Such recordings are available commercially, for example from the BBC, but are relatively expensive. You may be able to borrow some from the British Council library in your country.)

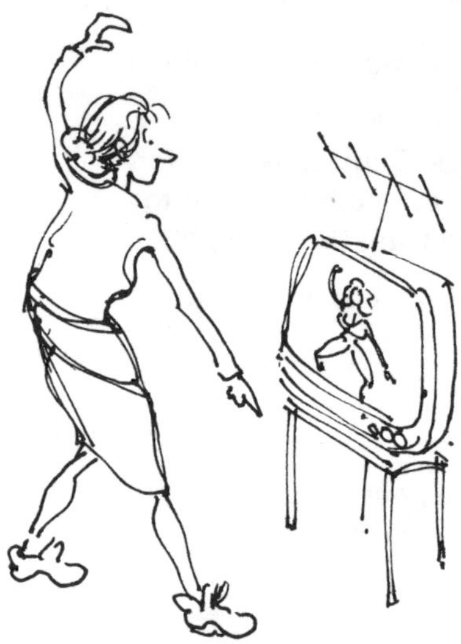

3 Pretend you have an English friend with you and have imaginary conversations with him/her. Remember to speak aloud, not just in your head.

4 'Shadow act' English-speaking people on television: as they are talking, try to imitate their gestures and body language. If you can, video-record a short sequence so that you can play it several times. Try to speak along with the TV person, imitating his/her pronunciation, intonation and pace.

5 Send letters to a penfriend on cassette - find a cassette-friend.

6 Get an English club going with colleagues or friends. Meet and talk together in English, for example over a meal in a restaurant, a drink in a bar or a coffee at home. Do some of the activities included in this book, e.g. *Just a Minute* (Unit 2), *Giving Talks* (Unit 4), *Reading Aloud, Interpreting.*

7 Try to find visiting native speakers, for example through the Lions Club, the Chamber of Commerce, etc. You may also be able to get in touch with visiting musicians and other performers. Offer your services as a guide or interpreter. Is there an organisation where you live that invites foreign visitors to meet local people?

8 Read as much English as possible for relaxation and pleasure.

9 Listen regularly to radio programmes in English, e.g. BBC World Service, Voice of America.

10 Find out what services (libraries, cultural programmes etc.) are available from organisations in your country such as the British Council, the American Cultural Centre, etc.

2 Visiting an English-speaking country

If your main reason for visiting an English-speaking country is to speak English with native speakers and through them get to know the country better, it will not be very useful at your advanced level of proficiency to spend a lot of time studying at an English language school. Instead:

– Take part in a holiday study course or volunteer work camp on a topic that interests you, e.g. photography, music, walking, wildlife, literature, sailing, the theatre, archaeology, arts and crafts, gardening, history.

– Find a job, for example as an 'au pair' in a family.

(Note: EC (European Commission) nationals may work in Britain without a work-permit (with the exception of Spanish and Portuguese nationals, who require work-permits until 1993.) Nationals from non-EC countries can rarely do paid work for they would require work-permits, which are extremely difficult to obtain. Au pair work is the exception: a work-permit is not needed, providing a letter of invitation from the family can be shown at the port of entry into Britain.

Work permits are not usually required for volunteer workcamps and charitable projects. However, it is advisable to get entry clearance to Britain before you leave home, from the British Embassy or British diplomatic post in your country.)

The addresses and booklets listed below will help you find out more about holiday courses, workcamps, and jobs in Britain.

1 National Institute of Adult Continuing Education (NIACE)
(England and Wales)
19B De Montfort Street
Leicester LE1 7GE

Tel: (0533) 55145

The NIACE publishes, twice yearly, a booklet, *Residential Short Courses*, which gives the dates and addresses of courses on an enormous range of topics including jazz, murder mystery weekends, history, batik printing, bird watching, the Vikings, literature, karate, lacemaking, sculpture, spinning, science and ESP, bookbinding, table-setting design, astronomy, personal growth, picture framing, gliding, folk dancing, yoga, etc. etc.!

During the year, most of these courses are only for two or three days at weekends, but at Easter and in the summer (July - August) there are longer one, two and three week courses.

2a) Field Studies Council (England and Wales)
Preston Mountford
Mountford Bridge
Shrewsbury SY4 1HW

Tel: (0743) 850674

2b) Scottish Field Studies Association
Kindrogan Field Centre
Enochdhu
Blairgowrie
Perthshire PH10 7PG

Tel: (025081) 286

The Field Studies Council and the Scottish Field Studies Council run weekend and one-week courses on various aspects of nature-studies and ecology.

3a) Youth Hostels Association (England and Wales)
Trevelyan House
St Stephen's Hill
St Albans AL1 2DY

Tel: (0727) 55213

3b) Scottish Youth Hostels Association
7 Glebe Crescent
Stirling FK8 2JA

Tel: (0786) 72821

Both Youth Hostels Associations run residential courses in the summer, and sometimes at Easter. Many of these are activity courses, e.g. sailing, walking, climbing.

4) Council for British Archaeology
112 Kennington Road
London SE11 6RE

Tel: (071) 582 0494

Details of archaeological excavations for which volunteers are needed are listed in the Council's bulletin *British Archaeological News*, issued March to September and November and January.

5 Scottish Community Education Council
Atholl House
2 Canning Street
Edinburgh

Tel: (031) 229 2433

Their annual information sheet, *Summer Opportunities*, lists addresses of volunteer projects in Scotland.

6 Quaker International Social Projects
Friends House
Euston Road
London NW1 2BT

Tel: (071) 387 3601

At Easter and in the summer, this organisation conducts workcamps staffed by volunteers, almost half of whom are from outside the UK. Camps may involve manual work (e.g. decorating, gardening), children's holidays and playschemes, work with handicapped people, and other social projects.

7 Vacation Work
9 Park End Street
Oxford OX1 1HJ

Vacation Work publishes annually several very helpful books with contact addresses and general information: *Summer Jobs in Britain* (includes addresses of au pair agencies); *Adventure Holidays*; *The International Directory of Voluntary Work.*

8 Central Bureau
Seymour Mews
London W1H 9PE

The Central Bureau publishes annually *Working Holidays*, witn information about short-term jobs in Britain, Northern Ireland, Eire, New Zealand, Australia, Canada, USA (and many non-English-speaking countries).

2.3 Reading aloud - Task 3

Student A

£350,000 PAID FOR LUCKY CAR NUMBER PLATES

HONG KONG: Law Tingpong, a textile tycoon, has paid £350,000 for one of the colony's most treasured possessions - a car number plate. The world record price was paid at auction for the single figure 8, prized by the superstitious Chinese because the Cantonese word for eight sounds like the word for prosperity. The locals in one of the world's most materialistic societies always associate the number with riches and good luck. 'I was prepared to pay anything for it,' said Law, 75.

11 YEAR OLD AVIATOR FLIES ACROSS THE ATLANTIC

LE BOURGET, France - Eleven-year-old aviator Christopher Lee Marshall landed yesterday at Paris Le Bourget airport, becoming the youngest pilot to cross the Atlantic.

Christopher started his flight July 7 in San Diego. He was accompanied on his trip by retired U.S. Navy pilot Randy Cunningham, 46, who limited Marshall's flying time to eight-hour stretches.

The transatlantic venture included stops in St. Louis, New York, Montreal, Greenland, Iceland and Scotland. Christopher arrived Wednesday night in Glasgow after a 1,350 kilometre flight from Reykjavik, Iceland in his single-engine Mooney 252 aircraft.

Christopher's mother said her son began flying with his father when he was four years old and began training with an instructor when he was seven.

CONGO EXPLORER CLAIMS 'DINOSAUR LIVES'

A FAMILY of dinosaurs may still be alive in the Congo, two US scientists said in Dallas, Texas, yesterday. Mr Roy Mackel of Chicago University, and Mr James Powell, a Texas-based zoologist and explorer, said that the theory was based on witness accounts given to them on an expedition to the Congo and on reports of earlier explorers.

MUSICAL MICROCHIP MUG NOW ON SALE

THE LATEST novelty for Christmas is a tea mug with a microchip hidden inside. It plays a tune when you pick the mug up. The system works with light, as explained in European patent application 240 591 from a Japanese company, Origin.

A small battery, musical synthesis chip and tiny loudspeaker are potted in translucent resin underneath the mug. There is also a phototransistor. When the mug is lifted, light triggers the transistor, switching power through to the musical chip.

Aspirin 'could prevent strokes'

MORE THAN 1,500 strokes a year could be prevented if stroke patients were given a daily dose of aspirin after their first attack.

A conference on the treatment of strokes held in London last week, the findings of which are to be published in the *British Medical Journal* on Friday, reported that if stroke patients were given half an aspirin a day after their first attack, the chances of a second stroke could be reduced by a quarter.

1.1 *Balancing on the edges of language - Task 2*

Part A

Breaking the rules of language is something we all readily associate with literature. So when Dylan Thomas writes *a grief ago*, using an abstract noun where we'd expect a noun of time, the unexpected sequence of words makes us sense a nuance of meaning that the word does not have in isolation. *All the moon long*, writes Thomas, in another poem, and again, a new utterance is born. Such creation doesn't come easily. 'Every English poet', said Robert Graves, 'should master the rules of grammar before he attempts to bend or break them'.

But it's not just poets who carry out linguistic manipulation. Theologians do the same thing, as they strive to express in human language their perception of something which transcends humanity. In the past 30 years, the main trend in the language of theology has been to find new ways of bending language to say illuminating things about God - at one extreme, resulting in a radically new language of prayer, as in this verse from 'Litany for the Ghetto':

O God, whose name is spick*
black-nigger*, bastard, guinea* and kike*,
Help us to know you...

There's even a new branch of linguistics devoted to it - 'theolinguistics', it's called. And a book by an American theologian, Paul van Buren, is called *The Edges of Language* (SCM 1972).

Poets? Theologians? Hardly the stuff of every day. But in fact, as we walk down a street, or watch television, the bending and breaking of linguistic rules is all around us. Advertising is the most noticeable field.

Children of today play hard - and they have to eat hard too:
Kellogg's Corn Flakes. That's how you can eat sunshine every day...

And this ad will remind you of someone (see above):

Only two Alka-Seltzers ago
You were feeling down-hearted and low.
Who would ever know you were under the weather
Only two Alka-Seltzers ago?

The famous Heineken series of advertisements, in the early 1980s, show how rule-bending can become a truly creative process, extending over several years. The original ad read: 'Heineken refreshes the parts other beers cannot reach', and the picture showed some person or thing being relaxed after a drink of the beer. Later texts bent the rules further, and played on the word 'parts'. One ad said: 'Heineken refreshes the parrots other beers cannot reach', showing a picture of a sea-dog's parrot being revived. Another replaced 'parts' by 'pilots', showing an airliner scene. Another used 'pirates'. Imagine arriving in London and seeing the ad 'Heineken refreshes the pirates other beers cannot reach'? Inexplicable, unless you knew the original slogan.

* Slang used to refer to different racial groups. Often used as terms of abuse.

1.1 *Balancing on the edges of language - Task 4*

A's jokes

Take it in turns to read your jokes to each other. You have jokes 1, 3, 5, etc. **B** has 2, 4, 6, etc.

1 A Knock knock.
(B Who's there?)
A Ivor.
(B Ivor who?)
A Ivor you let me in the door or I'll climb in the window.

3 A Knock knock.
(B Who's there?)
A Arthur.
(B Arthur who?)
A Arthur any more biscuits in the larder?

5 A Knock knock.
(B Who's there?)
A Luke.
(B Luke who?)
A Luke through the keyhole and you'll see.

7 A Knock knock.
(B Who's there?)
A Wilma.
(B Wilma who?)
A Wilma supper be ready soon?

9 A Knock knock.
(B Who's there?)
A Alec.
(B Alec who?)
A Alec I nice cup of tea in the morning.

11 A Knock knock.
(B Who's there?)
A Scot.
(B Scot who?)
A Scot nothing to do with you.

13 A Knock knock.
(B Who's there?)
A Olive.
(B Olive who?)
A Olive here so let me in.

unit 2

1.1 Balancing on the edges of language - Task 5

A's jokes

Take it in turns to read jokes to each other. You have the first one. Wait for **B**'s question before you read the punch-line.

1 What is the longest word in the English language?
'Smiles' - because there's a mile between the first and last letters.

3 What goes up a drainpipe down but can't go down a drainpipe up?
An umbrella.

5 Why can't two elephants go swimming at the same time?
Because they only have one pair of trunks.

7 What begins with P and ends with E and has millions of letters?
The Post Office.

9 Why shouldn't you go out when it's raining cats and dogs?
You might step in a poodle.

unit 3

1.1 Telling anecdotes - Task 2

A's outlines

Use these outlines to tell two anecdotes.

1 A millionairess kept a pet mongrel dog that she was very fond of. Unfortunately it sometimes used to bite her visitors. Most of the dog's victims, anxious not to offend the millionairess, tolerated the animal. One friend, however, had had enough and told her friend that the dog had just bitten her again and should be got rid of. The millionairess refused: He loves me and he doesn't know how rich I am.'

2 The Earl of Halifax, former ambassador to the United States, was travelling in a train with two strangers: two rather prim-looking middle-aged ladies. The journey passed in silence until the train entered a tunnel. In the darkness, Halifax placed a number of noisy kisses on the back of his hand. As the train emerged from the tunnel, he turned to the ladies and asked: 'To which of you charming ladies am I indebted for the delightful incident in the tunnel?'

2.3 Reading aloud: stories

Group A's extract

From *Three Men in a Boat* (by Jerome K Jerome)

(*Three Men in a Boat* tells the story of three young men who go on a boating holiday together.)

We are very fond of pineapple, all three of us. We looked at the picture on the tin; we thought of the juice. We smiled at one another and got a spoon ready.

Then we looked for the knife to open the tin with. We turned out everything in the hamper. We turned out the bags. We pulled up the boards at the bottom of the boat. We took everything out on the bank and shook it. There was no tin-opener to be found.

Then Harris tried to open the tin with a pocket knife, and broke his knife and cut himself badly; and George tried a pair of scissors, and the scissors flew up and nearly put his eye out. While we were dressing their wounds I tried to make a hole in the thing with the spike end of the hitcher, and the hitcher slipped and jerked me out between the boat and the bank into two feet of muddy water, and the tin rolled over, uninjured, and broke a tea-cup.

Then we all got mad. We took that tin out on the bank and Harris went into a field and got a big sharp stone, and I went back into the boat and brought out the mast and poised it high up, and gathered up all my strength and brought it down.

It was George's straw hat that saved his life that day.

2.3 *Reading aloud: letters - Task 1*

Letter A

Read this letter, from Qatar in the Middle East.

Dear Attractive Petite Blonde,

I have just received my copy of 'Private Eye' and was interested in your ad.

I am about to return to the UK to spend my summer leave and after another year here will eventually return to south-east England. Having spent more than a year in an Arab culture with no knowledge of Arabic, I should very much like to be reintroduced to my own British culture.

I am 24, 1.8 metres (if that is important) and enjoy classical and jazz music, opera, theatre, etc. Other interests are many and varied but include bell ringing (campanology), Morris Dancing, travelling, eating, drinking (and cooking) – to name but a few.

I have no attachments, am a carnivore, don't smoke, do just enough exercise to stay healthy and won't be offended if turned down.

I shall be leaving Qatar on 16 June and returning on 26 August. During that period I would like to take a short trip in Europe, but currently have no travelling companions.

If you haven't discovered the right person, I would be pleased to hear from you at the following address in England.

Yours,

Peter

2.3 Reading aloud - Task 3

Student B

WOMAN WAITS THREE QUARTERS OF A CENTURY TO RECEIVE HIGH SCHOOL DIPLOMA

TESS TWIETMEYER waited almost three-quarters of a century to earn her high school diploma, but a computer that didn't believe she was born in 1893 made her wait a few weeks longer.

Mrs Twietmeyer, 94, of Tribune, Kansas, finally received her diploma in the mail when humans took over from a computer that rejected her because it had been programmed to recognize only birthdates in this century and wouldn't print her name on a list of grads.

MUSIC AND ENTERTAINMENT GIVEN TO ANIMALS IN THE LONDON ZOO

LIFE WAS BORING for residents at the London Zoo - mostly sleeping, eating and watching the humans. Then came David Shepherdson.

With calls of the wild piped into the gibbon cage, a cricket dispenser for the mongoose, and plans to give the orangutans their own sound-and-light show, Shepherdson is making sure that visitors aren't the only ones having fun at the zoo.

AP reports that behavioural enrichment at the 61-year-old London Zoo has been particularly successful for little gibbon monkeys, who usually have one mate for life and assert their territory by singing. The zoo's pair weren't as musical as they should have been until Shepherdson hung stereo speakers near their cage which play taped gibbon duets twice a day.

Thinking they have neighbours, the gibbons sing back.

SHAKESPEARE HAD 'EXTRAORDINARY' MEDICAL MIND

SHAKESPEARE, the acknowledged master of the English language, also had an extraordinary grasp of medical science, according to a new study just published.

In 37 plays, he mentions practically all the diseases and drugs of the day and some of his descriptions could not be bettered by any modern doctor, says Dr Aubrey Kail, author of 'The Medical Mind of Shakespeare'.

FRENCHMAN 'WALKS' ACROSS THE ATLANTIC

Frenchman René Bricka is recovering in hospital at Trinidad after 'walking' 3,750 miles across the Atlantic, from the Canary Islands to the Caribbean, in 64 days on 15ft polyester floats.

Bricka, 39, is suffering from extreme hunger, delirium and defective vision and has lost 44lb.

FREE LOZENGES FOR WOULD-BE COUGHERS IN OPERA HOUSE

COUGHING at Sydney's Opera House should be an unheard-of disturbance this summer: the opera house is distributing free lozenges at the door. AP reports that the coughdrops, donated by the manufacturer, would be given to all opera fans throughout July and August.

'For years concert-goers, critics and performers alike have been plagued by the constant interruption of coughing audiences,' said Robert Pool, spokesman for the Opera House Trust. 'Hopefully, this move will see an end to the cacophony of coughs during orchestral concerts and earn the opera house the title of a cough-free zone.'

1.1 *Balancing on the edges of language - Task 2*

Part B

Breaking the rules of language is something that happens continually in daily newspapers, especially in their search for memorable or eye-catching headlines. The most famous example is The Guardian, which makes a point of extracting the maximum meaning out of the ambiguities of language, using puns, rhymes, and all kinds of linguistic allusions. One issue (17 June 1986) gives us, in an article on the lead-up to the Spanish elections: 'The reign in Spain which dampens the electorate' (remember *My Fair Lady*? 'The rain in Spain falls mainly on the plain'? And, in what must be one of the worst puns on record, the same issue reports on a television programme about treasure-searching for opals in Australia, with the headline: 'When all seems opal-less'! (Get it?[1])

And what about television? Listen to any TV comedy programme, and you'll find what is probably the most difficult linguistic genre of all - the language of popular humour. And what is this largely based on? Linguistic rule-bending - incongruity, unexpected juxtapositions of words, puns, loaded meanings, and the like. A sketch about the British government at the time of a recent crisis, when one minister had resigned and another was likely to, included the line (spoken by Mrs Thatcher): 'I told you that two Ministers ago'[2].

Literature, theology, advertising[2], professional comedy...all bend rules. But actually the most creative domain of linguistic rule-bending is the amateur world of - everyday normal conversations. I was listening to a group of students talking in a pub a short time ago. The most noticeable feature of their dialogue was the way they would play with each other's language, 'being clever', for fun. ' T'ank you', said one, adopting a mock Irish accent, as someone brought him a drink. 'No tanks here', said someone else, making a literary allusion which made them all groan. Then, 'Time to make tracks', said a third, and they all collapsed into helpless giggling[3]. (They had been in the pub for some time, it seems.) I've heard similar repartee from people of all ages and all walks of life. Children begin experimenting with the processes involved as early as eight, torturing parents with their awful jokes.

Child: Knock, knock.
Parent: Who's there?
Child: Ken.
Parent: Ken who?
Child: Ken't (=can't) tell you!

[1] Hopeless', of course.

[2] When you discuss your text with **A**, s/he will be able to talk about this.

[3] 'Make tracks' - 'leave', but also, tracks can refer to the continuous belt enclosing the wheels of a tank.

2.3 Reading aloud: letters - Task 1

Letter B

Read this letter.

The holder of Box 000 is invited to join me for an evening at the Royal Festival Hall any mutually agreeable date next month.

I've just relocated in London after working in Warwickshire and previously travelling around the world, before settling down to a 'proper job'. So I am actively getting back to grips with all the nightlife which would make my evenings enjoyable (even allowing for potential personality clashes!); if you would like to have a look at the enclosed programme, I'm sure you could choose an evening that you too would enjoy.

I hope so: supper comes in with the deal by the way!

To give you the background: ex-Cambridge scholar, 23, tall, dark and handsome (it's all relative!), adventurous and wildly romantic (about special people) but most importantly, healthy and happy. I'm interested in theatre, cinema, music flying sports (as a participant), design and travel - but more so with other people.

You can get in touch with me out of office hours on the above number -

If I don't hear from you, best of luck with the other guys!

Stephen

1.1 Balancing on the edges of language - Task 4

B's jokes.

Take it in turns to read your jokes to each other. **A** has no.1, 3, 5 etc. You have 2, 4, 6 etc.

2 B Knock knock.
(A *Who's there?)*
B William.
(A *William who?)*
B Wiliamind your own business.

4 B Knock knock.
(A *Who's there?)*
B Toby.
(A *Toby who?)*
B Toby or not Toby, that is the question.

6 B Knock knock.
(A *Who's there?)*
B Shirley.
(A *Shirley who?)*
B Shirley I don't need to tell you.

8 B Knock knock.
(A *Who's there?)*
B Alison.
(A *Alison who?)*
B Alison to my radio.

10 B Knock knock.
(A *Who's there?)*
B Watson.
(A *Watson who?)*
B Watson television?

12 B Knock knock.
(A *Who's there?)*
B Isabel.
(A *Isabel who?)*
B Isabel really necessary on a bike?

14 B Knock knock.
(A *Who's there?)*
B Húgo.
(A *Hugo who?)*
B Hugo that way and I'll go this way.

unit 2

1.1 Balancing on the edges of language - Task 5

B's jokes

Take it in turns to read jokes to each other. **A** has the first one. Remember to ask a question so that **A** can give you the punch-line.

2 What did the hotel manager say to the elephant who couldn't pay his bill?
Pack your trunk and clear out.

4 What's the difference between a wizard and the letters K E M A S?
One makes spells and the other spells makes.

6 What's the best way to communicate with a fish?
Drop it a line.

8 What prize did the man who invented doorknockers win?
The Nobel prize.

10 What did the chimney-sweep say when he was asked if he liked his work?
It soots me.

unit 3

1.1 Telling anecdotes - Task 2

B's outlines

Use these outlines to tell two anecdotes.

1 During a visit to a small English town, Prince Philip (the husband of Queen Elizabeth) stopped to talk to two very old ladies. One of them boasted to Prince Philip that she was a hundred and four, and her friend was a hundred and one. Prince Philip smiled and replied that he didn't believe her because ladies always take ten years off their age.

2 The conductor, Thomas Beecham, had a friend called Utica Welles. When they were out walking one day, Beecham told her that he didn't like her first name and would like to change it. She said he couldn't - but he could change her surname. And so they were married.

2.3 *Reading aloud: stories*

Group B's extract

From *Memories of Childhood* by Dylan Thomas

'Fire!' cried Mrs Prothero, and she beat the dinner-gong. And we ran down the garden, with the snowballs in our arms, towards the house, and smoke, indeed, was pouring out of the dining-room, and the gong was bombilating, and Mrs Prothero was announcing ruin like a town-crier. This was better than all the cats in Wales standing on the wall in a row. We bounded into the house, laden with snowballs, and stopped at the open door of the smoke-filled room. Something was burning all right; perhaps it was Mr Prothero, who always slept there after midday dinner with a newspaper over his face; but he was standing in the middle of the room, saying 'A fine Christmas!' and smacking at the smoke with a slipper.

'Call the fire-brigade', cried Mrs Prothero as she beat the gong. There was no fire to be seen, only clouds of smoke and Mr Prothero standing in the middle of them, waving his slipper as though he were conducting.

'Do something,' he said.

And we threw all our snowballs into the smoke - I think we missed Mr Prothero - and ran out of the house to the telephone-box.

'Let's call the police as well,' Jim said.

'And the ambulance.'

'And Ernie Jenkins, he likes fires.'

But we only called the fire-brigade, and soon the fire-engine came and three tall men in helmets brought a hose into the house and Mr Prothero got out just in time before they turned it on. Nobody could have had a noisier Christmas Eve.

2.3 Reading aloud : letters - Task 1

Letter C

Read this letter from Newcastle.

Hallo there,

I read your ad in Private Eye with interest so thought I'd drop you a line. No doubt you are wondering why I should wish to contact someone in London. Well let me explain.

My name is Jim, I'm 35 and a journalist. Up to November last year I had spent the previous two and a half years working on various papers in the South - the last one being in Bristol.

I returned North to learn computer technology with a view to moving back South (hopefully to the London area).

Apart from classical music, I share your interests. I also enjoy travel, photography, reading and some TV.

I've had an unfortunate time in the past few years with my private life - but don't think I'm a beer-swilling, big spending neurotic. Far from it!

I am solvent, drink very little and (in spite of some unfortunate experiences) would like a lasting relationship with a lady. I do hope you will decide to contact me because I really would like to make a friend in the London area.

In case you think the distance is too great, I am fortunate to be on regular hours with weekends free at the moment. It's less than three hours from here by train so I would be happy to travel South.

I do hope you will decide to contact me and that we might eventually be able to arrange a meeting.

Yours sincerely

Jim

PS If you do reply, I will send you a photo next time round.

Introduction - Thinking about speaking

The main purpose of this *Introduction* is to help students clarify for themselves why they wish to improve their spoken English and what their specific aims are. Take care not to let the discussion go on for too long in any section, unless all the students seem truly engaged in it. Having started to think about their aims aloud in class, they will probably continue to think about them on their own throughout the course.

Quotations head every chapter and are intended for 'peripheral' reading, not for discussion in class. There is no need for you to draw the students' attention to them.

4 Working on your own

You could introduce the idea of 'repertoire' by asking the students what they would say if, for example, a friend was looking worried and they wanted to find out what was wrong. Build up a list of expressions on the board and ask the students which ones they tend to 'favour'. For example:

What's up (with you)?

What's wrong (with you)?

What's the matter (with you)?

What's / Is anything worrying you?

What's on your mind?

For homework, ask the students to read **About this book**, pages 5-10).

unit 1

USING LANGUAGE TO BE SOCIABLE

PART ONE

1.1 Encouraging conversation

The words missing from the tapescript are:

Yes, I've been there. / I could guess. / Was he right or were you right? / How embarrassing! / Like what? / *Oh, how* beautiful! / *Yes I have, it's* gorgeous. / *Oh no! I mean* what do you say *to that sort of comment?* / *Oh, they're* beautiful! / Gorgeous, *yes*. / As usual! / I don't belive it. / Good job, *though*.

1.2 Redirecting the conversation

In this unit, and throughout the book, many of the tasks are to be done in pairs or small groups. If you feel that this does not allow you to give enough feedback to everyone or makes it difficult for you to keep track of how the students are coping, vary the set-up sometimes. For example in 1.1 Task 3 or 4, or 1.2 Task 2, you could ask one group to talk while the rest of the class listens. Everyone can then participate in giving feedback to this group.

If you can, try to make a video recording of some groups for feedback purposes so that the students can experience this technique before they discuss error correction in 1.4.

1.3 It's not what you say, but how you say it

Task 1

The students should mark the intonation something like this:

1 Yes, dear. **3** Yes, dear.

2 Yes, dear. **4** Yes, dear.

The pace is quickest in 1 and slowest in 4.

PART TWO

2.1 Shadow reading : awkward encounters

If it is impossible for you to do Shadow reading, use the Shadow reading texts in all the units for additional reading aloud practice. Follow steps 1 and 2 in the Shadow reading procedure (page 6) and then ask students to practise reading aloud using the notation they have noted down from the recording. Allow them to listen to the recording again after they have done some practice on their own.

Task 2

To help your students identify their particular problems, you may find it useful to refer to *Learner English : a teacher's guide to interference and other problems* by M Swan and B Smith, Cambridge University Press 1987.

2.3 Reading aloud: news snippets

Instead of asking students to read the list of hints about reading aloud on page 8, you can introduce them to reading-aloud techniques yourself. Read this or any other text aloud and ask the students to notice the techniques you use. In addition to noticing intonation, pausing, and pace (which they can also get from a recording) they will notice how you lift your eyes from the page to keep eye contact with your audience, how you hold the book, and how you use gestures (for example, turning your head to indicate the location of different characters).

If necessary, discuss catenation with your students and explain that, in English, the end of one word flows straight on to the beginning of the next. (This is why non-native speakers sometimes feel that native speakers 'eat their words' or don't speak clearly.)

A particular problem students may have is when there is a vowel at the beginning of a word, particularly when the word is stressed. English speakers glide smoothly from the final sound of the word before to the initial vowel of the following word.

For example: Workers‿at‿a Hong Kong‿abbatoir ...

It will help students to think of the consonant as belonging to the next word. This will stop them making a gap before the vowel.

Sometimes the sound of a final consonant disappears when the following word has an initial consonant.

For example: refused‿to; knelt‿down; promised‿that.

For examples and exercises on catenation, consult texts such as J D O'Connor *Better English Pronunciation*, Cambridge University Press.

If the students have a lot of problems in reading aloud, you will have to supplement the exercises in this book with simpler exercises. For example they may need more practice in breaking up sentences into sense groups, in joining words (catenation), in reading a sentence silently and then looking up to make eye contact and reading it aloud.

The recording of *Tears Save Buffalo* could be used for 'listen and repeat' practice, pausing the tape in each breathing place.

ENJOYING LANGUAGE

1.1 Balancing on the edges of language

Task 4

All the jokes represent examples of 'tampering' with language. Students may like to discuss the nature of the tampering e.g. phonological, phonetic, dialectal, orthographical.

Key to the jokes:

1 Ivor (Either)
2 Williamind (Will you mind)
3 Arthur (Are there)
4 Toby (To be) or not Toby (To be)
5 Luke (Look)
6 Shirley (Surely)
7 Wilma (Will my)
8 Alison (I listen)
9 Alec (I like)
10 Watson (What's on)
11 Scot (It's got)
12 Isabel (Is a bell)
13 Olive (I live)
14 Hugo (You go)

Task 5

Play the example on the cassette and ask students to repeat the Feed question. While the students are reading the jokes in pairs, check that they are using the correct rise-fall intonation in the Feed question.
Some students may need help in understanding some of the jokes:

1 sMILEs
2 trunk = elephant's nose/large suitcase
3 An umbrella is 'up' when it is open and 'down' when it is closed
5 trunks = elephants' noses/swim wear
6 'drop someone a line' = 'write someone a letter'; 'a line' can also mean 'a fishing line'
8 Nobel/'no bell'
9 poodle = type of dog; puddle = pool of rain water
10 'soots' could be a verb made from the noun 'soot'; it has the same pronunciation as 'suits'

1.2 Idioms

Apart from teaching students some vocabulary and idioms that may be new to them, this can be a useful dictionary exercise with students using a range of dictionaries to discover which ones are the most useful in helping them to find the meanings of idioms.

The idioms that have been confused are:

1 to come full circle
(according to) the swing of the pendulum

2 to smoke like a chimney
to drink like a fish

3 to put one's money where one's mouth is

4 to have another string to one's bow
(to have another feather in one's cap)

5 to be over the moon about something
to be on top of the world

6 to cut one's teeth on something
to get one's teeth into something

1.3 A game : Call my Bluff

Give each group about four or five words. You can select from this list, or find your own.

grayling	gabble	douse	cocky	petty	pong
poop	poppycock	quash	quip	rigmarole	rickety
scrimp	plover	ripple	rumple	rutted	sapling
saunter	shun	twitch	vouch	wobble	wangle

Some of the preparation of both true and false definitions can be done for homework, with students writing out definitions as they might be found in a dictionary. Group members can then compare their definitions in class and select the ones they are going to use for the game.

Students should be able to get into the spirit of the game quite easily. However, if any groups have problems, you could show them these examples, created by students during the piloting of this book.

Gabble

1 Informal. Used to refer to a man who is a fence-sitter, who finds it hard to make up his mind. e.g. *He is such a gabble! He must miss a lot of things in life.*

2 Informal, N. Fast talking that is very difficult to understand. Also V. e.g. *He gabbles so much that I can't understand a word.*

3 Informal, V. to turn upside down. N. a mess
e.g. (mother to child) *What a gabble in here!*

1.4 Expressing yourself without words.

Task 1

The actors on the cassette are using Scenario 4.

2.2 Word study : coined words

The underlined words were all coined by Lewis Carroll.

'Twas <u>brillig</u> and the <u>slithy</u> <u>toves</u>
Did <u>gyre</u> and <u>gimble</u> in the <u>wabe</u>;
All <u>mimsy</u> were the <u>borogroves</u>,
And the <u>mome</u> <u>raths</u> <u>outgrabe</u>.

'Beware the <u>Jabberwock</u>, my son!
The jaws that bite, the claws that catch!
Beware the <u>Jubjub</u> bird, and shun
The <u>frumious</u> <u>Bandersnatch</u>!'

He took his <u>vorpal</u> sword in hand;
Long time the <u>manxome</u> foe he sought -
So rested he by the <u>Tumtum</u> tree,
And stood awhile in thought.

And as in <u>uffish</u> thought he stood,
The <u>Jabberwock</u> with eyes of flame,
Came <u>whiffling</u> through the <u>tulgey</u> wood,
And burbled as it came.

One, two! one, two! And through and through
The <u>vorpal</u> blade went <u>snicker-snack</u>!
He left it dead, and with its head
He went <u>galumphing</u> back.

'And hast thou slain the <u>Jabberwock</u>!
Come to my arms, my <u>beamish</u> boy!
O <u>frabjous</u> day! <u>Calloo!</u> <u>Callay!</u>'
He <u>chortled</u> in his joy.

'Twas <u>brillig</u>, and the <u>slithy</u> <u>toves</u>
Did <u>gyre</u> and <u>gimble</u> in the <u>wabe</u>;
All <u>mimsy</u> were the <u>borogroves</u>,
And the <u>mome</u> <u>raths</u> <u>outgrabe</u>.

unit 3

STORY TELLING

PART ONE

Before starting the exercises in Part 1, the students may wish to discuss the art of good story-telling and some of the verbal and non-verbal 'tricks' that are used by good story-tellers. They could also attempt to analyse the 'tricks' of some well known TV or radio personality who often tells anecdotes or stories.

1.1 Telling anecdotes

Task 2

You may wish to supplement or substitute the written anecdotes given here with ones that you have found in a local newspaper or magazine. If these are in the students' mother tongue, this does not matter: this introduces an element of interpreting practice into the exercise.

1.3 Discussing stories

As well as bringing others into the discussion, students should try to make use of phrases they have already practised to encourage others to continue speaking (Unit 1) and to interrupt politely (this unit).

PART TWO

2.2 Word study : sounds

Students should use dictionaries to find associations for the words they do not already know. This part of the exercise could be set as homework.

2.3 Reading aloud : stories

If your students are studying to become teachers of English, you can use texts from an English textbook that students will teach in the future instead of using the two texts given here.

2.4 Interpreting : a visit to Scotland

If it is not possible for students to do this exercise in a language laboratory, an alternative is to make a few copies of the recording and have the students work in small groups with a tape recorder for each group.

GOING SOLO

1.1 Giving talks

While thinking about talks they have given, the students may also find it interesting to think about some of the similarities and differences between giving a talk and telling an anecdote or a story.

If the 'clustering' technique of brainstorming ideas is new to the students, build up another example on the blackboard by writing a topic in the centre of the board and adding students' contributions.

How informal the students' talks are will depend on what is most appropriate for your students to practise. The main aim of the exercise is to give students an opportunity for transactional language practice, in a long uninterrupted turn.

1.2 Making a speech

Task 2

The expressions on the cassette are:

Opening remarks
Good afternoon, ladies and gentlemen.
I'm delighted to be with you this afternoon.
It gives me great pleasure to introduce this afternoon's speaker.
I'm here today to tell you something of the work I have been doing.

Summing up
So, to finish I'd just like to say how much we have enjoyed the visit.
In conclusion, ladies and gentlemen, I'd like to say ....
May I say, once again, what a great pleasure it has been to be with you this afternoon.

Thanking
On behalf of my colleagues, I should like to thank the catering staff for looking after us so well.
I should like to take this opportunity to say thank you to our speaker.
I'm very grateful for all that you have done for us.
I am delighted to have been asked to propose a vote of thanks to all the staff.

Task 3

Point out to the students that they should not use all the information given in the notes about Timothy Locke. Rather, they should pick out what is relevant. You may wish to supplement the situations given here with ones that are more relevant to your students. You may also wish to invent information about other speakers based on the model given here.

1.3 A game : Just a Minute

Remember to bring a stop-watch to the lesson!

PART TWO

2.2 Word study : clichés

Some of the clichés in the text are rarely used (e.g. 'prefer the grape to the grain') or are old fashioned. Use also depends on factors such as sex, age and background of the speakers and their relationship with each other. Good modern dictionaries will give students some guidance as to the currency of some of the clichés. However, it is probably safe to say that the students should avoid using them themselves, at the risk of sounding rather odd.
Here is the conversation without the clichés:

Derek Hallo, Eric, I haven't seen you for a long time.
Eric Ah, Derek! Care to join me? What would you like?
Derek Well, since you insist...!
Eric What'll you have then?
Derek Some red wine, if you don't mind.
Eric You prefer wine to beer, eh?
Derek I've got to watch my heart.
Eric (confidentially) I'll just call the barman... Barman! A glass of red wine for my friend.

(The barman gets the drink.)

Derek How is your wife?
Eric Mary? Very well indeed. Mind you, she spends far too much time at home watching TV and smoking cigarettes. (Pause) I had a very nasty experience at the weekend, Derek. (The barman brings the red wine.) How much is that?
Barman One pound ten.
Eric There you are. Anyway, there I was, driving along, pretty fast, when a motorcycle came off a roundabout at a terrific speed. All of a sudden it looked as if my end had come.
Derek You thought you were going to get killed.

Eric And how! I slammed on the brakes, I did - and just missed the bike by an inch. I'd nearly hit him. Fortunately the police weren't in sight. So I got really furious with him. Told him he ought to be a bit more careful. And left it at that.

2.4 Interpreting : at the British Museum

Before students do this exercise, you can ask them to predict some of the vocabulary that may be used. They can then think of how to translate these words into their own language. They may predict some of these words:

> to mummify, brain, lungs, intestines, afterlife, to be reborn, bandages, pyramid, tomb.

If it is not possible for students to do this exercise in a language laboratory, an alternative is to make a few copies of the talk and have the students work in small groups with a tape recorder for each group.

DEBATING

1.1 *What is a debate?*

Task 2

Students should have no problem in identifying the more formal of each of the expressions or recognising them on the cassette. The correct answers are:

1b, 2b, 3a, 4a, 5b, 6a, 7b, 8a, 9b, 10b.

They may, however, feel reluctant to use such formal expressions when addressing their fellow students in the debate. It will then be necessary for you to remind them that the essence of a debate is its formality, both in its procedure and its language.

1.2 *Preparing a debate*

Note that each group is working on a different motion. This means that, in each debate, the audience will come fresh to the topic that is being debated.

If it is not possible to conduct several debates over a series of lessons, you will of course have to arrange the groups differently. For example you may have groups of eight prepare each debate with two students working on each speech. Only one student will deliver the speech.

If there is time for only one debate, allow the four speakers to prepare their speeches in their free time. Do not engage the whole class in preparation, for this will destroy the freshness of the debate itself.

1.3 *The debate*

If necessary, remind students of the formal language that they looked at in 1.1 Task 2.

2.4 *Interpreting : summarising from the newspaper*

Students can use the English newspaper items in Unit 1 (pages 80 and 86) to do a second task, interpreting from English into their mother tongue.

1.3 A chatathon

Stage 1

It is assumed in the procedure described here that you will have to use students as judges. However, it will be much better if you can recruit people other than students from your class to help out as judges: other English teachers, English-speaking friends, students from other advanced classes. This will allow all students to take part in all the conversations in Stage 1 - and make the competition a real chataTHON! For the same reason, it is better if you are the Controller, rather than one of the students.

You may be able to arrange for a combination of student and 'outside' judges. In this case, try to plan the groups so that conversationalists are judged an equal number of times by their peers and by 'outside' judges.

If you have to use students as judges, you will have to plan the groups carefully for Stage 1 so that students all take part in an equal number of conversations. (It does not matter if they do not all act as judges an equal number of times.)

To save time on the competition day, explain the competition *Procedure* and discuss the *Guidelines for judges* in the preceding lesson. How many conversations you are able to have in Stage 1 and exactly how long each one lasts will depend on your particular situation. Try to plan for all students to take part in at least 3 (but preferably more) conversations. Stages 2 and 3 can be conducted the following lesson.

It is important that the students do not know the conversation topics in advance and that the topics do not assume background knowledge that some students may not have. Below are some suggestions, which you can add to. The topics are deliberately broad, so that the conversationalists can deal with them in any way they like.

Favourite places
People I admire
Books
Relatives
Exams
Learning English
Pop stars
The power of the media
Waste

Stages 2 and 3

As only four students will be conversing in Stage 2, students can act as judges. In Stage 3 you may wish to bring in 'outside' judges to make the judging more objective and give the competition more status.

Note: It may interest students to know that this chatathon competition is derived from two competitions held annually in Britain as a fund-raising event by the Association for Spina Bifida and Hydrocephalus. Competitors are asked to find sponsors.

One competition is for people over 18, the other for people between 15 and 18. Stage 1 lasts a whole day and competitors take part in sixteen twenty-five minute conversations. On the second day there are 'knock out' quarter and semi finals and the final. Conversations for the older age group last one hour, for the younger group half an hour. The final conversation is judged by a panel of celebrity guests. The prize for both competitions is a trip for two in a significantly named 'hot-air' balloon!

PART TWO

2.4 Interpreting : radio and TV news

Before the lesson, record a TV and/or a radio news bulletin. For Tasks 1 and 2 the bulletins should be in the students' mother tongue. For Task 3 the bulletins should be in English.

If you are using a TV news bulletin, students can sit close to each other in pairs and interpret quietly to each other.

If you are using a radio bulletin, students can do the tasks individually in the language laboratory or using cassette recorders in the classroom.

Introduction

1 A student talks about her spoken English

Wanda So, what I think about my English. I'd like to improve it a lot because um I think I, there are many words I don't know and I'd like to know them because I, I like the colloquial expressions and er the way people speak naturally and and I'd like to, yes to be able to, to repeat those expressions, That's why I have a notebook and whenever I can, I note them down, those expression, these expressions, these idiomatical expressions, and I try to repeat them afterwards and to place them into a conversation. And um, it's also because I, I would like to pass for an English woman, er, and and to be completely one of them, because I, I like the language very much and the country too and the way people live and I, I like to understand them better and I think through language it's, it's very interesting and it's a good way because then you can, you can have er talks with every kind of people. I'd like to have a perfect pronunciation because I don't think I, um, I make the good stresses and er sometimes people make me repeat, have me repeat and that's obviously not the the right pronunciation I have used and er I like so much no, no-one could distinguish me from or just er hear that I'm not English, because it's a beautiful language.

Unit 3

2.4 Interpreting : a visit to Scotland (3' 55")

Right. So you have two and a half days to visit Scotland. Not very long, is it? Um, and I suggest the first day stay in Edinburgh and in the morning go on a coach tour of the city, just for, for half a day, just for the morning, and on the coach tour you will see the castle, Edinburgh castle, which is very beautiful indeed, very impressive, and then from there you'll go past the cathedral, St Giles cathedral, and then on down to the palace, Holyrood Palace. So that'd be the castle, the cathedral and the palace, just from the coach. And then the coach goes through the what we call the New Town, on the north side of Edinburgh, that, it's not new, it was built in the eighteenth century, but anyway it's called the New Town. Then from there the coach goes to the zoo and, it'll just pass the zoo, and it goes on outside the city in fact to two bridges that are over the River Forth, that's about ten miles from Edinburgh, two bridges, one is a road bridge and the other is a rail bridge, for trains. And then the coach will come back from the bridges, back into the city and it will leave you in the city centre. So that's the morning. And I suggest in the afternoon that you go back to the castle and you spend the afternoon walking around the castle, there's a lot to visit in it and er the view also is wonderful, you have a wonderful view and in fact the view, in the view you'll see the New Town that you saw in the morning and you can just see one of the bridges also that you will have seen in the morning from the coach, on the coach tour. So that's the first day. The second day I suggest you take a coach tour outside the city, a whole day coach tour, and there's a lovely one that goes, it leaves about nine in the morning I think, half past eight or nine, we'll check on that, and it goes right across Scotland to the west coast to a town called Oban, that's O-B-A-N, Oban, and the journey is beautiful, it goes through lovely countryside so, if the weather's nice, you'll have lovely views, and in Oban you then take a boat and a boat, there's a boat that goes to an island called Shiel Island and um, it's just very nice you know to get out of the coach, have a bit of sea air and if you're lucky on the boat trip you should be able to see some seals as well. And then the coach will get back to Edinburgh about nine o'clock in the evening. So it's, it's quite a long day but well worth it. And then on the third day, well you'll only have the morning, so I suggest you spend the morning shopping, er, you can buy lots of woollens of course in Edinburgh, sweaters and things like that, tartans, if you want to buy some Scottish tartans, um and any souvenirs that you that you want to get, so I suggest you spend the morning shopping. And then the train back to London leaves at two o'clock in the afternoon and that's about a five-hour journey so you'll be back in London about seven o'clock in the evening. So I hope you have a very good trip indeed.

Unit 4

2.4 Interpreting : at the British Museum (2′ 51″)

John Reeve If you come to the British Museum any day of the year the rooms that you'll find most crowded are the rooms that have the Egyptian mummies. People seem to want to see dead bodies from the past and they seem particularly interested in seeing the wrapped up bodies of the ancient Egyptians. What you did was to take something rather like a coat hanger and stick it up the nose and remove the brain. You then opened up the body down the side and took out the lungs, and the liver and the stomach and the intestines. And because you needed all these when you were er reborn in the afterlife they produced four pots, four special jars, to put the lungs, the liver, the stomach and the intestines in, each with the head of an animal or a person on it so you knew which was which. They then cleaned out the body and packed it with a sort of dry salt so it didn't rot and they washed it down and put all sorts of sweet smelling things on it like perfume and then you wrapped it up rather like a lot of bandages in linen. When you'd finished doing up the bandages, you then lay the body inside a painted box the shape of a body without arms with a head at the top and covered in pictures of what they thought would happen to the body in the afterlife. And then it was laid inside another big box and then possibly inside another big box and then it went into a tomb, perhaps under one of the pyramids if it was a Pharaoh. Today with the help of modern medicine we can do X-rays on mummified bodies and we can even work out how some of these ancient Egyptians died, for example there's one mummy which has very jagged teeth marks at the ends of the knees, and no lower legs at all, and the mummy was found to be very wet, very waterlogged, and they think that this person probably fell off a boat in the Nile and was attacked by a crocodile and then when they mummified the bodies they made up legs out of linen to make it look like a whole body.